Copyright © 2014 by Dennis L. Cerrotti

All rights reserved. No part of this publication may be reproduced, stored in a retrieval system, or transmitted in any form or by any means, electronic, mechanical, photocopying, recording or otherwise, without prior written permission of the author or publisher.

Sea Venture Press
58 Russell Road
Wellesley, MA 02482

First Printing – April, 2014

Hidden Genocide

Hidden People

by Dennis Cerrotti

Contents

Preface	I
Historical Chronology	III
Map of New England	V
Prologue – Hidden Genocide	1
Chapter 1 – The Roots of Genocide	13
Chapter 2 – The Theology of Encroachment	34
Chapter 3 – The Pequot Massacres	52
Chapter 4 – The Spoils of War	81
Chapter 5 – Religious Imperialism	101
Chapter 6 – The King Philip War and Genocide	129
Epilogue – Hidden People	156
Index	167
Photo Gallery	172

Preface

Much of my curiosity about Native Americans originated during my childhood in Connecticut. Like most places in New England, Connecticut is adorned with some of the last vestiges of Native American culture – Algonguin words. Indeed, so many Algonquin words adorn the linguistic landscape of New England that words such as Connecticut, Massachusetts, Narragansett, Mohegan and others are so ubiquitous as to seem English, in a sense. As a young person, that fact did not elude me as being especially significant, given the reality that the people who originated the beloved vocabulary were curiously absent. Why? That is the question I try to answer here.

As most people are aware, there is a certain primitive aspect to the idea of Native Americans in our culture. That is particularly true in New England, where the word "savage" was often used even in official communications. It was intentional. Throughout the centuries, Native Americans were typically portrayed as having deserved their fate, doomed to extinction as another superior race of people took their place. But as history proceeded forward, new ways of interpreting the unsettling narrative of genocide in America have been created, particularly through the mass media. These new approaches have been helpful, and they have often led to important revisions in the historical narrative concerning Native Americans, their civilizations and cultures. With this book, I hope to contribute to that narrative by examining the 'heart of darkness' which pervaded Puritan attitudes toward Native Americans in their religious life.

There have been many people, scholars, friends, family and people I've met along life's journey who have helped me research and finish this book. I would be remiss not to mention one first, my life partner and wife, Janet Seckel-Cerrotti. Without her encouragement and interest in this subject, it would have been so much more difficult, if not impossible to engage the topic in a comprehensive fashion. That meant innumerable trips and stops along the roadside, visits to sites, testing of ideas, review of texts, and proofreading and much more. I could go on, but I will instead mention here my children, Rebecca, Rachael and Jesse, all of whom have had to endure my obsessive interest in this topic. That is said in good humor, for each of them, now adults, have been supremely helpful in proof-reading, cover design and other elements of my work. Muchas gracias!

Like many historians, many of my theories are dependent upon the research, insights, support, and work of others in the field – too many to cite here. But there is a list of people I especially want to personally acknowledge. Most importantly, I would thank one my professors from twenty years ago, Dr. Beth Norbeck from Andover Newton Theological School. It was her guidance and suggestions which led me to this topic in a focused way, and it resulted in a dissertation on the topic of Native Americans and Puritans. In many ways, the research I completed for that project has formed part of the background for this new book.

Besides scholarly research, significant field research forms the basis of this book. I want to acknowledge with gratitude the late Slow Turtle (John Peters), Supreme Medicine Man of the Wampanoag nation, who graciously gave of his time to educate me, both through a formal interview and several conversations on the topic. In addition, I especially thank Nina Olff for her support and insights on the topic. The many hours we spent in the field together engaged in research and conversation were invaluable and enjoyable.

There were several people whose help in editing and improving the text was of the highest order. They deserve my deepest thanks for all that they were able to do to make it readable and comprehensible. In particular, I want to thank Ruth Sharpe, whose language and editorial skills are only surpassed by her deep knowledge of history and law. Without her help in articulating difficult and complex subjects, this book would undoubtedly still be a 'work in progress'. In addition, I want to thank Peter Golden, one of the most knowledgeable historians and writers in the Boston area for his help in many ways, but especially in reviewing some of my text and helping to create the synopsis. Finally, but not least, I want to thank Oriane Piskula, for her yeoman's work in proofing the text and for her suggestions and ideas. It was a true honor and priviledge to have such incredible and knowledgeable people beside me in the long journey toward understanding and the difficult, yet rewarding process of writing this book.

Historical Chronology

1616   Estimated starting date of a severe epidemic of an unknown disease affects Native Americans in Massachusetts and Maine with well over 50% casualties from the disease.

1620   The first permanent English settlement in New England is established at Plimoth by separatist Puritans (Pilgrims)Within a year, Pilgrims enter into a pact with the Pokanoket Wampanoags.

1623   Second English colony called Maremount established at Quincy, Massachusetts by a group led by Thomas Morton. The settlement is highly successful, particularly in trading activities.

1625   Persecution of Separatists and Puritans in England increases when Charles I takes the throne.

1628   Plimoth attacks Maremount following accusations that Thomas Morton and his followers were engaging in paganistic practices. Morton is left stranded on an island off the Maine coast, but is later rescued by Native Americans. He returns to England to initiate a lawsuit to terminate religious control of New England.

1629   A Royal Charter is granted by England to the Puritan sponsored Massachusetts Bay Company, giving it limited rights to settle and govern the land around the Massachusetts Bay.

1630   Over 1,500 non-separatist Puritans settle Massachusetts Bay. John Winthrop is chosen as the first governor of the colony.

1631   Rev. Roger Williams is offered the post of Teacher in the Boston church, which he refuses on the basis that the church is not separated from the non-Puritan Church of England.

1632   Roger Williams accepts an appointment to become Assistant Pastor in Plimoth. There, despite pressure by the Massachusetts Bay leaders to cause his removal, he advocates strongly against occupying Native American land without purchase. He is later forced to flee to Salem and eventually to Rhode Island.

1635   Waves of English Puritan settlers led by Rev. Thomas Hooker travel by land and boat to illegally settle Connecticut.

1636   After a difficult midwinter journey through snow and cold, Roger Williams and several companions end their journey at Providence where the Narragansetts welcome them and offer them land.

1637   The Pequot War in Connecticut results in genocide.

1644   The Narragansetts, at the urging of Rhode Island settlers, declare their submission to the King of England.

1646   Missionary work under the direction of John Eliot coincides with a period of harsh persecution of Native Americans.

1661   Osamaquin (Massasoit), Sachem of the Pokanoket Wampanoags dies. His son, Wamsutta, becomes new Sachem at Mount Hope.

1664   Wamsutta mysteriously dies en route to Plymouth after being forced there by English authorities. His brother, Metacomet (known as King Philip), becomes Sachem.

1671   Metacomet is interrogated concerning rumors that the Wampanoags are secretly planning to war against the English.

1675   A brutal war breaks out between the Wampanoags and English (King Philip War). The colony of Rhode Island and the Narragansett nation declare neutrality, but English forces massacre large numbers of Narragansets in a surprise attack during winter.

1676   Metacomet is killed at Mount Hope. Many houses in Providence are burned after Indian rebels warn Roger Williams and the residents to leave their homes in advance. English troops defeat and massacre large numbers of Wampanoags, Nipmucs, Narragansetts and others. Most captured survivors are either enslaved or executed.

1683   Roger Williams dies during winter. The precise date of his death is unknown.

1684   Original charter for Massachusetts Bay is revoked by the King of England.

A map of Native American nations (or tribes) according to 17th century English sources. This is a partial list, and is but one version of many differing accounts and renderings from the initial "First Contact" phase of European exploration.

Prologue
Hidden Genocide

What makes New England history different from others? The answer is simple – theology. The most cogent place to begin a study of Native Americans and Puritans in the seventeenth century is to examine the role of theology and the way in which it impacted Native Americans. Of course, some might suggest another point to begin with valid justification, such as the roles of technology, disease, war, politics or culture in the early colonies. All approaches have their value in a wider context. But, in New England, theology nevertheless reigned supreme, more powerful than cannon and gun, and more powerful even to the point of usurping the royal laws and enactments of England. Even more importantly, theology was the lens through which Puritans often defined and described Native Americans, their culture and customs. Therefore, it would be difficult to assess and analyze the motives and rationale of the relationship which developed between Europeans and Native Americans without turning to theology. This is an important distinction, for American history is often understood and communicated without detailed reference to religion or theology, and many history textbooks ignore the topic of theology completely. By sequestering such a large volume of material evidence, a great disservice is rendered. Because theology did play such a key role in the culture, public policies, record keeping, sermons, letters, tracts and a host of other literature from the period, it is an important key to understanding more completely the history it impacted.

In New England, we must also remember that most public discourse was theological, whether explicit or implicit, and that most people were highly superstitious. The Puritans were incessant sign seekers and believers in omens, and this often tipped over into outright paranoia when it came to Native Americans or non-conformist English settlers. Any crisis or catastrophe could be linked to something else, typically perceived sins or failures, depending upon the strength of association or correspondences. In turn, these perceived threats to the social order were responded to with iron-fisted policies which utilized torture, death and humiliation as the primary social constraints. While draconian policies were embraced by many tyrants of the time, this is particularly true in New England, an experiment in theocracy that quickly revealed its profound limitations and fatal consequences to those who dared to resist its unjust demands. Yet, in the course of winning their battle against Native Americans and non-conformists, the Puritans lost the war for their own survival. In this book, theology will be the link to our past as a means to explore its more subtle complexities, and more importantly to inform our future.

The Puritans conceived a form of government that would be based on the concept of religious covenant. For Puritans, the idea of the covenant determined who was and who was not a Christian, with a strict standard that devalued and punished those who did not conform to the Puritan model. In this model, clergy had the power and influence to prescribe moral and legal standards and punishments, but it was the civil order which enforced its laws, disciplines, and doctrines with the power to punish violators, including those who came under the criticism or condemnation of the church. Thus, it was the civil government rather than the church in Massachusetts that banished or persecuted people such as Roger Williams, Thomas Morton, Mary Dyer, Anne Hutchinson and countless other non-conformists for heresy, rather than an ecclesiastical court. This was a significant departure from European practice and the Roman Catholic inquisitions, but the results were similar. The ecclesiastical investigation of Anne Hutchinson's views and the arrest order for Roger Williams at the insistence of Boston clergy, for example, demonstrate the workings of this rather unwieldy system. From the beginning, the rigidity of such legal systems put many under duress for beliefs and practices that under English common law were considered normal and legal. The Puritans devised a way to merge the workings of state and church into a rigid, unyielding structure built primarily to take charge and maintain order within the colony.

Under the system, it was the civil government's responsibility to declare and conduct war when needed, but it was the clergy's role to provide a theological rationale for wars and other policies of the government. Clergy were also expected to accompany soldiers in battle and provide encouragement and support, as required by the first unofficial set of laws, often referred to as the "Cotton Code",[1] written by

---

[1] John Cotton, "An Abstract of the Laws of Massachusetts," in The New England Way, ed. Sacvan Bercovitch, (New York: AMS Press, Inc, 1984), 17.

Rev. John Cotton from the First Church of Boston. It must also be noted that the Cotton Code, while never enacted in its original form by Massachusetts Bay, was later adopted by the New Haven colony.

In the end, the Puritans of New England were drawn together by the exalted idea of a religious covenant and body of laws and restrictions which would extend beyond the local congregation and into the private, public and secular domains. Despite this rigid authoritarian scheme, in the end the Puritans struggled unsuccessfully for a way to unite the inner workings of government and church which would reflect their vision and still appease the government in England. Eventually, their failure would be felt in the waves of discontent which swept across New England, the results of acrimony, disputes and a draconian approach to law and order. Almost immediately upon receiving the initial charter, and before any settlement had been established by the Massachusetts Bay Company, the Puritans were planning to defend their independence and dominion in New England by asserting a theological mandate based upon a typological description of their mission and community. "We shall be a city upon a hill, and all the eyes of the world will be upon us," famously intoned John Winthrop, asserting the Puritan willingness and enthusiasm to boldly plant their flag in the new world, determined that the best means to that end would be through the creation of a theocratic form of government. But this concept was controversial among many English leaders, and led to much tension and acrimony between the colonies and the royalist government. Many Puritan leaders rose to the occasion of defending the infant Puritan colonies in sermons, tracts, and letters. In a letter defending the newly-established order in Massachusetts, John Cotton explains some of its particulars and nuances:

> It is better that the commonwealth be fashioned to the setting forth of Gods house, which is his church: than to accommodate the church frame to the civill state. Democracy, I do not conceyve that ever God did ordeyne as a fitt government eyther for church or commonwealth. If the People be governors, who shall be governed? As for monarchy, and scripture, yet so as referreth the soveraigntie to himselfe, and setteth up Theocracy in both, as the beste forme of government

in the commonwealth, as well as in the church.[2]

The intensity of Puritan belief in the righteousness of their cause in New England was strengthened by their sense of involvement in wars against the Native Americans. The key to understanding this doctrine in New England Puritanism is typology.[3] Typologically, New England was the 'New Canaan' based upon the old Canaan depicted in the book of Exodus. Like the account in Exodus, in which Hebrew tribes warred against the settled population of Canaanites, the Puritans believed that their violent struggle to gain physical and legal possession of Native American land was not only divinely ordained, but also of even greater ultimate importance than the biblical Exodus, which was interpreted as a pale shadow of the glorious kingdom to be established in New England. This is the beginning of American millennialism, a theological movement that is still potent today, especially in Christian fundamentalism. We find an example of this popular Puritan belief in Edward Johnson's Wonder-Working Providence :

> For Christ the great King of all the Earth is now going forth in his great Wrath and terrible Indignation to avenge the bloud of his Saints, Ezek. 38 and 19. vers. and now for the great and bloudy Battell of Gog and Magog, Rivers of bloud, and up to the Horse-bridles, even the bloud of those have drunke bloud so long. Oh! dreadfull day, when the patience and long-suffering of Christ, that hath lasted so many hundreds of yeares, shall end. What wonderous workes are now suddenly to be wrought for the accomplishment of these things! Then judge all you (whom the Lord Christ hath given a discerning spirit) whether these poore New England People, be not the forerunners of Christs Army, and the marvelous providences which you shall now heare, be not the very Finger of

---

[2] John Cotton, "Copy of a Letter from Mr. Cotton to Lord Say," in The New England Way, ed. Sacvan Bercovitch, 415.

[3] Typology is a predictive methodology in the field of Christian theology, using data, history and metaphors from the Bible to determine the creator's will or plan for specific groups of people, in this case the Puritans and the Native Americans.

God, and whether the Lord hath not sent this people to Preach in this Wildernesse and to proclaime to all Nations, the neere approach of the most wonderful workes that ever the Sonnes of Men saw. [4]

However, preaching in the wilderness was not the primary purpose of the mission, although it certainly played a central role in the espoused purposes of the New England Bay Company. The forerunners of Christ's army were warned before departing England for America that the spiritual battle would be waged with the physical weapons of war in order to battle the powers of darkness in the "wildernesse" of America. Thus the Puritans saw themselves as having received a very specific and special calling, one which was distinct from their Calvinistic European counterparts in practical measure, yet similar in terms of theological content. William Simmons describes their world view:

They saw the world as an arena where forces of light and holiness, represented by Protestant saints, fought against armies of sin and darkness, represented by devils who motivated aristocracies and priesthoods, and infiltrated the Christian community through immoral and undisciplined persons. This mental framework for comprehending evil both within and outside themselves provided Puritan colonists with a theory for interpreting cultural differences between themselves and the native people whom they encountered in the New World.[5]

Eventually, their zeal for the mission blinded the Puritans to the inherent contradiction between "preaching in the wilderness" and "avenging the bloud of the saints." In New England, resources for missionary activity were consistently and overwhelmingly outstripped by the amount of expenditures for armaments. Surrounded by enemies and competitors in America, it must have seemed logical and neces-

---

[4] Edward Johnson, Johnson's Wonder - Working Providence, in <u>Original Narratives of Early American History</u>, J. Franklin Jameson, ed., (New York: Charles Scribner's Sons 1910) 60.

[5] William S. Simmons, "Cultural Bias in the New England Puritan's Perception of Indians", William and Mary Quarterly, 38, no. 1 (Jan, 1981) : 56.

sary to embellish their rhetoric with violent imagery and establish the kingdom of Christ at the point of a gun. Of course, this type of zealotry has had countless precedents in Christian history. New England Puritanism can even be considered in the mainstream of "just war" theory. Therefore, a sense of theological certainty, combined with paranoia over their physical safety in New England, impressed upon Puritans the need to fortify their communities themselves with the physical means to undertake the demanding and risky task of conquest. Thus, Johnson gave this advice to those who were about to undertake the great journey into the new Jerusalem in America:

> You shall with all diligence provide against the Malignant adversaries of the truth, for assure your selves the time is at hand wherein Antichrist will muster up all his Forces, and make war with the People of God: but it shall be to his utter overthrow. See then you store your selves with all sorts of weapons for war, furbish up your selves with all sorts of weapons for war, furbish up your Swords, Rapiers, and all other piercing weapons. As for great Artillery, seeing present meanes falls short, waite on the Lord Christ, and hee will stir up friends to provide for you: and in the meane time spare not to lay out your coyne for Powder, Bullets, Match, Armes of all sorts, and all kinde of Instruments for War: and although it may now seeme a thing incredible, you shall see in that Wildernesse, whither you are going, Troopes of stout Horsemen marshalled, and therefore fayle not to ship lusty Mares along with you, and see that with all dilligence you incourage every Souldier-like spirit among you, for the Lord Christ intends to achieve greater matters by this little handfull than the World is aware of; wherefore you shall seeke and set up men of valour to lead and direct every Souldier among you, and with all diligence to instruct them from time to time. [6]

Despite the elaborate preparations for military engagement, it would be misleading to conclude that the Puritans came to New Eng-

---

[6] Johnson, <u>Wonder-Working Providence</u>, 33.

land solely to war against the Native Americans. Puritan leaders consistently held up the evangelical ideal of conversion, perceiving themselves in competition with Jesuit missionaries who had been long at work in Canada and along the Maine Coast. Gov. John Winthrop, in a letter written while still in England, heralded the contribution which the planned settlement would mean for the church. He writes, "It will be a service to the Church of great consequence to carry the Gospell into those parts of the world, to help on the comminge of the fullnesse of the Gentiles, & to raise a Bulworke against the kingdome of Ante-Christ wch the Jesuites labour to reare up in those parts."[7]

Nevertheless, the Puritans, although espousing a fervent desire to evangelize, did not commit the necessary resources for even a start-up effort until the 1640's with the creation of the Society for the Propogation of the Gospel, a group financed mainly by wealthy patrons in England. It is noteworthy that even this effort was in part motivated by the growing number of advertised successes of both French and Spanish missionaries in the Americas. Understandably, given the contentious atmosphere in European religious and political circles at the time, the English, while embarrassed at their own lack of effort, responded with both derision and disgust at these reports. "The Spaniard boasteth much of what hee hath already done in this kind, but their owne Authors report their unchristian behaviour especially their monstrous cruelties to be such, as they caused the Infidels to detest the name of Christ," chided William Castell in his original petition to establish the Society.[8]

To more fully understand the Puritan penchant for and success in battle against Native Americans, one must understand the role of superstition and myth in their theology. For example, one of the most important national myths which derive from seventeenth century New England is the concept of the righteous empire, a term popularized by historian Martin Marty. The myth of the righteous empire is rooted in Puritan theological claims and beliefs, and it would be impossible in a study such as this to ignore them. The Puritans were habitual theolo-

---

[7] Robert C. Winthrop, Life and Letters of John Winthrop 1588-1630 (Boston: Tecknor and Fields, 1864), 309-310.
[8] William Castell, A Petition of William Castell Exhibited to the High Court of Parliament (1641), (Northhampton: Taylor & Son 1882), 8.

gians in the sense that they seemed to find religious meanings and mystical portents in everything from the most commonplace occurrences to the most scholarly concurrences. In other words, it did not take much in the way of coincidences or logic to convince a Puritan. The tendency to find mystical correspondences between the ancient Jews and their own civil sphere falsely reassured them that their god was in some way purifying their commonwealth, setting it apart, raising it up and, in so doing, condemning to death the ancient civilizations which preceded them in New England.

In some ways, it is difficult to penetrate the guile found in Puritan literature. Much of it is pompous and provocative, reflecting a toxic combination of xenophobia and self-righteous attitudes toward non-Puritans. The Puritans, in ascribing such exalted value upon their mission in the wilderness of America, naturally enjoyed and encouraged writing about themselves, their communities, and their experiences, and we are fortunate to have available countless letters, documents, and publications from the period. But while English literature is abundant from the period, there are few authentic Native American voices preserved within it. Only English writers such as Roger Williams, Daniel Gookin and a few others seemed to have had enough regard for native culture to have recorded any accurate information about it. Therefore, one must conclude that the real guile is not so much in the rhetoric as in the absence of it.

A central tenet of New England Puritanism was the conviction that their god had called them forth to create a community of their god's own people in the new world. United in religious covenant, they compared and identified their cause with the ancient Hebrews of the Old Testament and their exodus out of Egypt. There were many similarities suggesting this mystical identification. The most obvious comparisons were the flight from persecution, the passing over the sea, and the inhabitation of a land filled with heathen people. Being their god's own people would require dominion over what they understood to be a bleak wilderness populated by savage heathens. Taking upon themselves the mantle of responsibility, and believing in themselves as the "forerunners of Christ's army." In this, the Puritan leaders never doubted their entitlement to use every means possible to achieve dominion in New England.

Prologue

The lack of credible evidence on the Native American side leaves much of the recorded history of early colonial New England in doubt. It would be so much easier to interpret the events and character of colonial New England with the authentic voices of Algonquin speakers and writers, but those voices have been scantily preserved. In the struggle for dominion, the Puritans failed to record most of the basic features of the Algonquin culture and civilization they were rapidly displacing. What history they did record was highly prejudiced and colored by their religious views, political needs, and cultural values. The lack of attention to the true qualities of Algonquin culture by the earliest settlers is greatly magnified in the lack of awareness by present-day inhabitants of New England. Part of the reason is obvious. The myths obscure the reality. Over time, the maligned projection of the mythological "Indian" or "savage" was inculcated upon the national consciousness, and the record of conquest was covered over with a veneer of self-righteous rhetoric. Students of American history are typically and simply taught that the Pilgrims and those who followed after in colonial New England were brave and righteous heroes.

American historians rarely portrayed the New England colonists as invaders until the twentieth century, generally ignoring the fact that within fifty seven years of English permanent settlement in southern New England, autonomous tribal rule was systematically destroyed through encroachment, legal repression, and war. There is no evidence that the Puritans saw themselves as invaders, but much that they saw themselves as benefactors. This is the great irony of that age, that those who practice tyranny could be so deluded themselves as to believe their evil actions a reflection of the divine will. Great efforts were made by Puritan clergy to justify on a legal and moral basis any reason to prosecute a war or require submission to English laws, and most portrayed such events as fully favorable to the English, while Native Americans consistently remained blameworthy, even when blatantly innocent.

There are many complicated factors which explain the gaps in the historical record. While many English colonists developed close and even amiable relations based on trade and mutual assistance with Algonquin communities and individuals, there remained a deep gulf of suspicion, fear, and ignorance between the two cultures in general. The English consistently misinterpreted Native American culture, preferring instead to impose negative meaning even upon those aspects of it which appeared most benign and complimentary.

Somewhat ironically, many especially transparent examples of the tendency to ascribe negative meanings to Algonquin culture can be found in the writings of Roger Williams, a close ally and friend of the Narragansetts and Wampanoags in southern New England. He was also intimately acquainted with the language and customs of the Narragansetts and Wampanoags, and was one of the foremost observers and interpreters of Algonquin culture in his day. His work, <u>A Key to the Language of America</u>, is undoubtedly the most complete and objective source of ethnographic data of seventeenth century New England. Nevertheless, Williams' observations, though often complimentary of Algonquin culture, were highly prejudiced by his own cultural and religious values and beliefs. As a result, some of his descriptions seem inept and even supercilious today. In the following passage, he introduces and narrates an encounter between himself and a Narragansett father:

> Their affections, especially to their children, are very strong; so that I have knowne a Father take so grievously the losse of his childe, that hee hath cut and stobd himselfe with griefe and rage. This extreme affection, together with want of learning, makes ther children sawcie, bold, and undutifull. I once came into a house, and requested some water to drinke; the father bid his sonne (of some 8. yeeres of age) to fetch some water: the boy refused, and would not stir; I told the father, that I would correct my child, if he should so disobey me, &c. Upon this the father took up a sticke, the boy another, and flew at his father; upon my perswasion, the poor father made him smart a little, threw down his stick, and run for water, and the father confessed the benefit of correction, and the evil of their too indulgent affections.[9]

The tendency of all English writers to assign negative attributes to Native American culture was greatly increased by suspicions and

---

[9] Roger Williams, <u>A Key into the Language of America</u> (1643) (Providence, RI: The Roger Williams Press, 1936), 29-30.

frequent hostilities between the two cultures. In the earliest period of settlement, previous to the first Puritan conquest (Pequot War), a cautious yet seldom hostile sentiment toward Native Americans prevailed. Indeed, many early writers, like Thomas Morton, expressed sincere sorrow for the Native American losses from the great epidemic. Of course, many Puritans saw their demise as divine intention, and some even interpreted the calamities as absolute proof that their god was clearing the way for Puritan settlements in the region. By the King Philip War, the rhetoric had reached the heights of invective, while prescribing the course of genocide as the completion of their god's will toward 'heathen' Native Americans.

For the New England Puritans of the seventeenth century, the presence of ancient Native American civilizations created an ideological quandary. Justification for the usurpation of native habitation and political autonomy was based both on ethnocentric and theological principles. If the English hesitated at all in the conquest of New England, it was largely due to the question of legal prerogative. Questions that today may appear ethical or moral never seemed to intrude into the question of how best to subdue the Native Americans. In a sense, the real Native American did not really exist in the English mind, except as as a negative myth created by their religious imagination.

The devaluation of Algonquin culture by ascribing negative and even demonic characteristics to it was a key element in building a theology of conquest in New England. This is obvious across a wide spectrum of Puritan literature of the period, as well as in subsequent centuries in many different guises. Eventually, the negative myth became increasingly secularized, though the theological underpinnings were still there beneath the surface. Indeed, it was the same negative myth which echoed repeatedly throughout the later centuries when westward expansion progressed with little consideration for the many other tribes of America, just as it had in New England. Always, the negative myth prevailed, providing ready rationale for abuses, persecutions and genocide of Native Americans. Thus this mythical "Indian", born in the Puritan religious imagination in the guise of Canaanites, Philistines, Edomites and other ancient enemies of the Hebrew people, has gone through many reiterations and reincarnations in America. Regretfully, the impact of the myth has remained the same over the course of centuries – an ideological construct based upon the myth of European superiority and, in the case of the Puritans, based upon their self understanding as the chosen people of their god. One does not have to analyze this in great depth to understand its implications; the role of the mythical "Indian" as the antagonist in the imagined replay of the biblical exodus is a tragic and troubling theme in our nation's history.

Chapter One
The Seeds of Genocide

> The whole earth is the Lords garden & he hath given it to the Sonnes of men wth a general Comission: Gen: 1:28: increace & multiplie, & replenish the earth & subdue it, wch was againe renewed to Noah: the end is double & natural, that man might enjoy the fruits of the earth, & God might have his due glory from the creature: why then should we stand striving here for places of habitation, etc, (many men spending as much labour & coste to recover or keepe sometimes an acre or twoe of Lands, as would procure them many & as good or better in another Countrie) & in the meane time suffer a whole Continent as fruitfull & convenient for the use of man to lie waste wthout any improvement? [10]

The above words, penned by John Winthrop or one of his associates before their departure for Massachusetts Bay in 1629, contain the key to understanding the history of genocide in New England during the seventeenth century. The passage contains a clear sense of divine mandate for the Puritans to appropriate lands in the region known today as 'New England'. On the surface, the words may seem benign, and merely a pious expression of faith in divine providence. However, at a deeper and more intrinsic level, the statement contains the seeds of genocide in its presumption that Native Americans had lost their divine right to the lands which their ancestors had occupied for thousands of years. Why? The Native Americans had allowed the land to "lie waste wthout any improvement", an odious and misleading statement at best. The assertion that Native Americans hadn't improved the land was preposterous, a fact belied by the countless reports and testimonies telling of prosperity and plenty enjoyed by

---

[10] Robert C. Winthrop, ed., Life and Letters of John Winthrop, (Boston: Tecknor and Fields, 1864) 309-310. This is a section from an undated and unsigned paper containing a list of considerations for the settlement of a New England plantation.

the people in this region. The fields were planted and the woodlands so expertly cultivated that Native Americans in New England were completely, securely and comfortably supplied with food, shelter and all the basic needs of life. Their horticulture, fishing and hunting activities were productive because they understood the ecology and lived within its limits. Thomas Morton, the famous founder of Merrymount, the successful colony in Quincy which rivaled the Pilgrim settlement in Plimoth for a few years, described the native people surrounding his settlement as fully self-sufficient, far beyond the measure of the average European of that day, writing: "If our beggars of England should with so much ease as they furnish themselves with food, at all seasons, there would not be so many starved in the streets."[11] Morton's words, of course, contradict the very basis of the Puritan contention that the land was wasted by Native Americans. The contention was a blatant lie, based on a combination of malice and ignorance with a nefarious end in mind. Puritans throughout the next several generations continued to employ this distortion of reality to justify the appropriation of Native American land, often without deed or purchase, eventually extending the mandate's meanings into a policy of genocide. For centuries thereafter and arguably into the present, that same distortion has driven countless Native Americans into the abyss of history, whether through war, impoverishment, disease or other means. This is why New England is so important for Americans to understand – not the positive, cozy myths of brave pioneers, but the brutal reality of the lies which undergird them.

Most unfortunately, the lie which the Puritans propagated is still believed by a large number of unsuspecting Americans today, who accepts the truncated and distorted versions preserved in historical records, legends and myths as facts. Ironically, many of these founding stories of colonial New England are presented as a kind of adornment or icon, rather than factual historical narrative. Taken in sum, few of the adornments or icons connect meaningfully to the hidden people mistakenly referred to as 'Native Americans', who were the original discoverers and colonizers of America, and who seldom are given credit for it. The fact remains to this day that few have been exposed to those

---

[11] Morton, Thomas, New English Canaan, ed. Jack Dempsey, (Stoneham, MA), 2000

sources available to correct these distortions. Almost all of us who were born here or who have lived here have been steeped in these founding myths, their outlines imprinted upon our culture, landscape and in homes every Thanksgiving and at every other occasion in which our colonial heritage is invoked, making the myth an omnipresent feature of our national identity. Nevertheless, that is where things stand, and it is the point from which the truth and facts must emerge.

First, we must begin with questions and try to reach answers. Why is the Native American perspective largely missing or misrepresented in historical narratives? Why is their very presence sometimes ignored, as if they were merely 'bit players' in one of the major social and political dramas in history? The telling of their history has been selective, unbalanced and biased in a way that sustains the basic rationale that John Winthrop and his company put forward even before they landed in America. We have very little in our possession, either written documents or material remains, that can fully describe the cultures and people who inhabited this land before the Europeans arrived to stay. Those documents that do strive for accuracy and objectivity, such as Roger Williams' book, A Key Into the Language of America, and Thomas Morton's New English Canaan, remain obscure or unknown to most scholars in the field. Both of these men were outspoken critics of Pilgrim and Puritan policies, and are ignored even to this day by many mainstream historians and textbooks. Finally, the most important and most ignored record we have are the descendants of the original people, and the collective memories and values transmitted through their ancestors, culture and communities, however much they have been lost, destroyed, altered and reinvented through time. There are many impasses in this research, and more questions are raised than answered.

There were many reasons for Puritan dishonesty, among them religious triumphalism and political guile. But there are also structural reasons, the results of removals, epidemics and wars, leaving few behind to record what actually happened to their people. Native Americans were largely dependent upon oral transmission of information, so when epidemics, forced removals and other events decimated their communities, the basic patterns of communicating and record keeping were typically lost. England, by contrast, was a chirographic culture, meaning that the technology and systems of writing and printing were highly developed among English people, ensuring that their version of events would endure. The fact that John Winthrop is one of the most quoted figures by presidents and other government leaders to this day testifies to the potency of this legacy. Literacy also enhanced economic development and allowed the English to systematize their government and religion, as well as perpetuate their culture down through the generations. Furthermore, the most critical aspect of literacy is that writing systems conferred legal authority arbitrarily to the English, putting Algonquin tribes at a strategic disadvantage from the beginning, unable to defend themselves from legal forms of oppression and encroachment. All of this meant power, the power to dominate, but also the power to alter people's understanding and perception of facts, events, and ultimately of history and reality itself. Both the Separatists at Plimoth and Puritans later based in Boston knew very well how to use this power to their advantage, an advantage which has been passed down to the present day.

A sense of presumed innocence combined with religious fervor bolstered the hubris of European settlers and explorers, even in the earliest first contacts in New England. Some of this can be attributed to ships, guns, swords, cannons and other technologies which made the march of conquest so effective. However, hubris requires more than a sense of military superiority, and much of the hubris among Puritans was fueled by a triumphalist theology which intensified the martial tendencies of European societies, traits which can be traced back to the Crusades and earlier. Although there are many similarities to other religiously-fueled wars, Native Americans were at a profound disadvantage compared to Europeans on many counts, especially weaponry. The Pilgrims and Puritans who settled New England believed their weapons were a sign of divine favor – they believed they were the "chosen people!" As a result, Europeans sought to take quick advantage of their military superiority, assuming their claims upon New England to be a divine mandate cast in the same theological mold as the ancient Hebrews in Canaan.

The Puritans, of course, were not the only Europeans imbued with the sense of divine sanction. It was widely understood among Europeans that America belonged to them and not the original people who settled here, even when those same people offered friendship and help to explorers and settlers. Beginning with the French explorer, Jacques Cartier in 1535, European explorers recorded sightings of hundreds upon hundreds of other European vessels (documented and undocumented) along the north Atlantic coast. Most were fishing vessels, including Portuguese, Basque, Spanish, English, Dutch, French, Swedish and more. Did they make substantial contacts with Native Americans? The simple answer is yes, and the best evidence for them are the epidemics which surged throughout North America during this period, effectively wiping out huge populations in a few decades. Along with the fishing fleet, other Europeans sailed the waters along the coast in order to explore and engage in trade with the Native Americans. The evidence for this activity is revealed in the fact that one of the great challenges the French government faced was registering and regulating trade, and collecting tariffs. By keeping the fishing grounds secret, taxes were avoided. The result of this secrecy was the veiling of a huge amount of historical and ethnographic information from the written record, but not all of it. Thus the question remains, what do we know and what does it mean?

There is evidence that the earliest European fishermen and explorers both befriended and took advantage of Native Americans in different ways. It is interesting to read from accounts such as George Weymouth and Samuel Champlain's, and their descriptions of convivial relations, including sharing music, feasting and mutual aid. Such reports ignore the dark side of early exploration, a period in which there was so much damage to Native American and English relations that English agents brought the matter repeatedly to the attention of Parliament and King James. Sir Ferdinando Gorges, as the principle founder of the Plimoth Company, reflected these concerns to both houses of Parliament, stating:

> ...that the mischief already sustained by those disorderly persons, are inhumane and intolerable; in their manners and behavior they are worse than the savages, impudently and openly lying with their women, teaching their men to drink drunk, to swear and blaspheme in the name of God, and in their drunken humor to fall together by the ears, thereby giving them occasion

to seek revenge. Besides, they cozen and abuse the savages in trading and trafficking, selling them salt covered with butter instead of so much butter, and the like cozenages and deceits, both to bring the planters and all our nation into contempt and disgrace; that they sell unto the savages, muskets, fowling pieces, powder, shot, swords, arrowheads, and other arms, wherewith the savages slew many of those fishermen, and are grown so able and apt, as they become most dangerous to the planters.[12]

During the early contact period, another activity of an even more egregious kind was also taking place in New England – kidnapping. Kidnapping of Native Americans in New England and the Canadian maritimes was a common practice, beginning with John Sebastian Cabot in 1497, who kidnapped three Mic Mac Native Americans to bring back to Europe as curiosities. Giovanni da Verrazzano, on his historic voyage in 1524, kidnapped a young boy from Massachusetts who never saw his home again. The cruelty of many early explorers was incredible, and we only have a small sampling of reports from the period.

The French explorer, Jacques Cartier, in 1535, spent a brutal winter with his crew near present-day Montreal suffering from the pangs of hunger and the scourge of scurvy. Without the compasionate aid of Iroquois villagers, who provided food and medicine to cure the scurvy, it is unlikely that the French would have survived their ordeal. Then, as Cartier and his crew were preparing to return to France, they hatched a nefarious plan, and boldly and unapologetically carried it out. Despite the generosity and the saving of their lives, Cartier had the audacity to kidnap the sachem of the village, Donnacona, along with four of his men, and then afterword lie to the sachem's people about it, telling them that the sachem and his men had come onto the ship voluntarily and had decided to return to France with the French. Cartier also promised the people that they would return the group of captives the next year. However, the captives did not survive to return, and Cartier

---

[12] Gorges, Sir Ferdinando, "Description of New England" in the Collections of the Massachusetts Historical Society, (Boston, 1837) 70

returned and lied to them again, explaining that the group of captives had chosen to stay in France.

One might ask, how could people of any conscience treat their benefactors with such contempt after the benefactors saved their lives? The question begs for an answer, especially considering how widespread kidnapping of Native Americans in New England and Canadian maritimes had become by the 17th century. Absence of shame or wrongdoing is typical in the early sources, not only regarding kidnapping, but also military piracy, cheating, murders, massacres and a host of other nefarious behaviors engaged in by Europeans against Native Americans. This suggests strongly that Europeans were prone to regard Native Americans as less than equal from the earliest contact period. The feeling must have been mutual, but European technology and weapons were quickly appraised by Native Americans as essential to their own survival. Distasteful as it must have been to them, this mutuality of shared interests through trading activities appears to have trumped whatever fears or misgivings they had toward Europeans.

Early records reveal interesting details, motives and important historical consequences resulting from kidnappings along the coast of New England. It must also be noted that kidnapped Native Americans were valuable to European explorers, not just as curiosities or slaves, but as valuable sources of information and assistance as translators and guides. Thus we can begin to understand some of the unusual accounts and stories found in early sources. One, in particular, concerns Captain George Weymouth, sailing as an agent of Sir Ferdinando Gorges in 1605.[13] During his historic voyage, Weymouth's crew kidnapped five Native Americans near present-day Rockland, Maine. One of this group was a man named Tisquantum, known to most people as "Squanto" (the same Squanto who later lived with the Pilgrims in Plimoth). Another one was a sachem named Tihanedo, the brother of Samoset (the first Native American to visit Plimoth). It has also been argued that Samoset himself was part of the captured group, but that has never been proven, nor has it been determined why Squanto was captured in Maine in the first place, since his home was at Pawtuxet (Plimoth, MA). Although Weymouth's men had to physically subdue the men

---

[13] Hoffer, Peter Charles, A History of Early America. The Johns Hopkins University Press, (Baltimore Maryland, 1944) p. 81

Hidden Genocide, Hidden People

in order to kidnap them, Weymouth's account states that the captives were well treated. In fact, Squanto was allowed to return to his Plimoth by order of Ferdinando Gorges by 1614. Then, in an ironic and fateful twist of events, we learn that this same Squanto was kidnapped again, this time on Cape Cod, along with twenty-six other Native Americans by an infamous slaver named Thomas Hunt. Hunt brought Squanto and the group of captives to Malaga, Spain and sold them as slaves, but crafty Squanto was able to escape and flee to England. Then, in a further ironic twist, Squanto was rescued by Friars in England, and returned for a second time to his homeland via Newfoundland. This time, however, he returned to find his village emptied by the mysterious epidemic of 1616-18, leaving him the lone representative of his people and ancestral home just as Pilgrim immigrants suddenly appear upon his people's lands.

Squanto's story is fascinating and filled with irony, and there are few figures in colonial history as well-known or iconic. Witness the recent blockbuster film, "Squanto", in which the Squanto is protrayed as a heroic figure of epic proportions. But here myth does not stand up to the reality. The truly transformative figure in the Pilgrim tale is actually Samoset. While Squanto's assistance was admittedly central to the survival of the Plimoth colony, it was Samoset who was most influential in the end. Samoset has so often been described by historians as a mere emissary on behalf of Massasoit, the famous sachem of the Pokenokets based at Mount Hope (Bristol, RI). But this conclusion is based on erroneous assumption, since Samoset is described only as a sachem from Mawooshen (midcoast Maine), who had contact with English fishermen on Monhegan Island. Following is the original account from Edward Winslow and William Bradford's well-known book detailing early Plimoth Plantation history, Mourt's Relation:

> Friday the 16th a fair warm day towards; this morning we determined to conclude of the military orders, which we had begun to consider of before but were interrupted by the savages, as we mentioned formerly; and whilst we were busied hereabout, we were interrupted again, for there presented himself a savage, which caused an alarum. He very boldly came all alone and along the houses straight to the rendezvous, where

The Seeds of Genocide

we intercepted him, not suffering him to go in, as undoubtedly he would, out of his boldness. He saluted us in English, and bade us welcome, for he had learned some broken English among the Englishmen that came to fish at Monchiggon (Monhegan Island), and knew by name the most of the captains, commanders, and masters that usually came. He was a man free in speech, so far as he could express his mind, and of a seemly carriage. We questioned him of many things; he was the first savage we could meet withal. He said he was not of these parts, but of Morattiggon and one of the sagamores or lords thereof, and had been eight months in these parts, it lying hence a day's sail with a great wind, and five days by land.[14] He discoursed of the whole country, and of every province, and of their sagamores, and their number of men, and strength. The wind being to rise a little, we cast a horseman's coat about him, for he was stark naked, only a leather about his waist, with a fringe about a span long, or little more; he had a bow and two arrows, the one headed, and the other unheaded. He was a tall straight man, the hair of his head black, long behind, only short before, none on his face at all; he asked some beer, but we gave him strong water and biscuit, and butter, and cheese, and pudding, and a piece of mallard, all which he liked well, and had been acquainted with such amongst the English. He told us the place where we now live is called Patuxet, and that about four years ago all the inhabitants died of an extraordinary plague, and there is neither man, woman, nor child remaining, as indeed we have found none, so as there is none to hinder our possession, or to lay claim unto it. All the afternoon we spent in communication with him; we would gladly have been rid of him at night, but he was not willing to

---

[14] The location of Morattiggon has never been identified, but certainly refers to some area in mid-coast Maine near Monhegan, where Samoset reports he had visited and learned English.

go this night. Then we thought to carry him on shipboard, wherewith he was well content, and went into the shallop, but the wind was high and the water scant, that it could not return back. We lodged him that night at Stephen Hopkins' house, and watched him.[15]

Why is the story of Samoset so important? The story reveals an intriguing pattern of English and Native American relations during the late 1500's through the early colonial period. The fact that Samoset was clearly comfortable walking into the English colony at Plimoth, though they were clearly uncomfortable and distrusting of him (they secretly held guard over him the first night of his visit), demonstrates that he probably had his own intentions, and neither controlled nor directed by Massasoit. It is also not clear that he was inferior in rank to Massasoit, although many historians assume that as well. The fact is that both men carried the same rank, that of sachem or sagamore. This is further evidenced by English activities along the Maine coast where Samoset played a role similar to that of Plimoth. Therefore, it is not accurate to accord Samoset the role of bit player in the drama that unfolded in New England. Instead, we must consider the facts on their own merits.

By 1623, Samoset appears to have left the southern Massachusetts region to return back home to Mawooshen, an area defined in early sources as located along Penobscot Bay in Maine, which is the major reason why there is so little written about him in early Plimoth sources. In 1623, we have an account of him being entertained at a dinner at Casco Bay near present-day Portland by an explorer named Christopher Levett, also in the employ of Sir Ferdinando Gorges. In Levett's account, however, Samoset's name is changed to Somerset. It appears that, like many Native Americans, the spelling and/or pronounciation of Samoset's name went through some changes, leading to confusion on the part of scholars. These gaps in the record obscured his important role, not only in Massachusets, but Maine as well. We continue to see this pattern of spelling changes continuing in other seventeenth century writers as well, such as John Josselyn's referral to Samoset at

---

[15] Edward Winslow and William Bradford, Mourt's Relation or A Relation or Journal of the Beginning and Proceedings of the English Plantation Settled at Plimoth in New England, J.K. Wiggin, (Boston 1865) 33

Plimoth using yet another variant spelling – "Summersant". But probably the most important variant comes in the earliest document we have containing his name, even before Winslow and Bradford would write their description of him. The document is a legal deed, conferred by him in 1625, to Rev. John Brown for a 200 square mile parcel of land at Pemaquid, including Muscongus Island. And how did he sign it? He used the name Captain John Somerset, Sagamore.[16] Of course, this title answers some questions, but raises many more questions concerning his role and importance in New England.

It was not unusual during the seventeenth century for English colonists and explorers to confer honorific titles upon Native Americans, so the "Captain John" affixed to Samoset's name here indicates that he was held in high esteem by the English, but not as an indication of military rank. Furthermore, his position as a sachem representing the people of Mawooshen in mid-coast Maine, shows how much esteem and authority he carried among his own people as well. There is room for speculation here, and one possibility is that he was an arch-sachem or "Basheba" since his homeland, Mawooshen, is where the lineage of leaders called the "Basheba" in the protohistoric years also lived and ruled. Whatever the case, there is no doubt that his influence was powerful, extending far beyond the border of Mawooshen as far south as southeastern Massachusetts. Furthermore, English sources reveal other enticing details about his importance and role in New England. Christopher Levett's report on his meeting with Samoset probably sums it up best, referring to him as "Somerset, a Sagamore, one that hath ben found very faithful to the English, and hath saved the lives of many of our Nation, some from starving, others from killing."[17] From Levett's words alone, we can easily deduce why Samoset was given the honorific title of "Captain John Somerset, Sagamore", stated on the Pemaquid deed.

It is clear that even before the great epidemic, some coastal Native Americans were not only open to the presence of English interests, but solicitous for it. Here again, we turn to Levett's report, who describes

---

[16] Publications of the Colonial Society of Massachusetts, Volume 6, 60

[17] Christopher Levett, A Voyage Into New England, William Sones (London, 1628) 102

[18] ibid, p. 104

the friendliness and desire of Saco Native Americans for him to establish a settlement in their midst, writing, "...the Sagamore of Casco and Qttacke, told me if that I would sit downe at either of those two places, I should be very welcome, and that he and his wife would goe along with me in my boate to see them."[18] This little passage is quite a historical tidbit – it sounds faintly reminiscent of a modern day appointment with the local real estate agent. What was the reason for this patronizing attitude? The French backed Tarratines were the reason, just as they were still the reason in Massachusetts in the 1620's. The number of deeds and patents issued to Gorges' agents confirms the fact. This in itself may have been the encouragement that Massachusett and Wampanoags would need to open up their own lands to the English, evidence that Samoset himself probably put forth before Massasoit for encouragement. What Samoset probably didn't know is that there was a world of difference between the Separatists at Plimoth and the libertine agents, fishermen and adventurists employed by Gorges' Plimoth Company.

Gorges never intended to have a direct involvement in the many activities and developments under his name in New England, having never actually visited it. Instead, he left it to others, probably the main reason his influence began to wane as Puritans began to establish a stronghold in Massachusetts. Through the course of a decade, he had had the opportunity to build strong relationships with Squanto and Samoset's brother, Tihanedo, both of whom had been kidnapped by Weymouth and taken back to England. Here, of course, we are at a loss to explain fully the extent of Samoset's personal dealings with Gorges' agents beyond the Muscongus deed and fur trading activities, but we can assume they were both substantive and transformational, including weapons and other technologies. We can assume that somehow amends were made over the kidnapping, as we have records that Samoset had personal dealings with some of the most powerful figures in early New England history, including Massasoit, Governor Edward Winslow, Miles Standish, William Bradford, Captain John Smith and Captain Christopher Levett. Undoubtedly, Sir Ferdinando Gorges was indirectly a major part of that equation, a role that would be bolstered in the following decades as emigration increased.

Reviewing some of Levett's report shows evidence for the above.

The Seeds of Genocide

First, Levett does not indicate any involvement in trading weapons, but his recorded observations show that guns and other technologies were already in circulation amongst Maine Native Americans. Levett also indicates that, upon his departure back to England, he would leave men behind at Saco with the explicit assurance from the Native Americans that the men would be welcomed. Why? Levett's words to Samoset and the other sagamores reveals the reason for their enthusiastic embrace of English settlers. He writes, "I would leaue of my men there until I came againe, and that they should kill all the Tarrantens they should see (being enimies to them) and with whom the English haue no commarsse."[19] So, in 1624, while the war was still engaged, it would appear that the influx of guns and the English presence had shifted the tide.

Another set of questions emerges from the above. Why did Samoset sell a portion of his people's holdings around Muscongus Bay? Was it for protection against Tarratines, or perhaps other motives as well? First, since the English-owned land bordered Mawooshen, it provided a buffer zone. By 1625, the date of the Muscongus deed, Samoset's people had already suffered two decades of war with the French-armed Tarratines. Though most history texts barely allude to the war, it was a much greater tragedy than the near silence on the subject would suggest. Historians C.H. Webber and W.S. Nevins described it as killing "thousands upon thousands", with the Tarratines displaying a brutality "scarcely paralleled in the history of human warfare."[20] The point here is obvious. Samoset must have regarded the growing presence of the English in New England as his people's best hope from being completely destroyed by the Tarratines. Second, by selling off a piece of Mawooshen land, Samoset was not only creating a buffer zone, but also establishing a legal right under English laws for his own people, not just of the new English owner. In later years, both rights of ownership were further protected and upheld in 1679 when descendants of the original buyer, Rev. Brown, were required by the courts to establish the chain of ownership, and they presented the original deed with Samoset's name and mark upon it. Thus a legal precedent was established which, at that date, recognized Native American ownership of Mawooshen. This legal

---

[19] ibid, p. 112
[20] Goffe, John, "Remembering the Tarratines and Nanepashemet", (Neara Journal, v. 39 #2), 2006

right later allowed it to serve as a refuge for those Native Americans fleeing after the King Philip War, as well as the later French and Native American wars as well. Arguably, Samoset had served his people's interests well by securing this legal right to Mawooshen, as it was the only Native American territory in New England to remain autonomous and under Native American control until around 1750.

There is nothing new in the theory that European greed, weapons and trade goods brought woes and destruction to the Native Americans of North America, much of it due to strategic imbalances brought about by the introduction of these commodities. The Tarratines were the first of many North American Native Americans to quickly adopt European technology, being the most eastward of Native American nations. Samoset was in a unique position to understand first-hand exactly what this influx of technology meant. Faced with the prospect of either English presence or continued Tarratine genocidal attacks, a choice had to be made. It is obvious that most sachems and sagamores in coastal New England had decided in favor of the English, if for nothing else, to acquire the guns and ammunition needed to fend off the Tarratines.

One of the mistakes American historians often make when it comes to New England is to underestimate the brutality and impact of the Tarratine war and its importance to later developments. Why? One reason is the lack of documentation, which is why most historians regard the period as proto-historical instead of historical. Most of the information has been gathered through second-hand sources. It is possible, however, to gain a clear picture of how European technologies, particularly sailing craft, guns and swords, grotesquely exacerbated the carnage exacted in the Tarratine war. One of the best sources for this is a French source, a poem written by Marc Lescarbot. Lecarbot was a French lawyer, poet and adventurer, as well as a close associate of Samuel Champlain. In the following excerpt from a long poem commemorating the war, Lescarbot provides vivid and gory details into the impact of European swords and guns in a 1605 invasion of the French supported Tarratines, led by the sachem Membertou, against the Saco Native Americans at Saco Bay, a community closely aligned with Mawooshen:

> The Armouchiquois (Saco Indians), seeing that it

was all over for them if they did not promptly put their trouble right. ...They were for the most part armed with knives which they were accustomed to wear around their necks, but these weapons were of little use at this time because Membertou (and his men) were equipped with good armor with a shield of hardwood and a good cutlass. Just as the swing of a scythe lays low honor in fine epics, his sword likewise reaped the enemy with extreme rapacity. The others carried away with a like ardor, following the chief's pace do not lack courage, but with cries and frightful voices kill these poor wretches like ants. ...Two muskets (for which he likes the French very much), ...with their blows ten of them fell dead and the noise of this thunder frightened the rest. [21]

In contrast to the bloody images portrayed in Lescarbot's poem, we find a quite different description of traditional Native American warfare portrayed in Roger William's book, A Key Into the Language of America. It is important to make the comparison here in order to demonstrate the horrific effects which the introduction of European weapons had upon Native Americans in this region. He writes:

Their wars are far less bloody and devouring than the cruel wars of Europe; and seldom are twenty slain in a pitched field, partly because when they fight in a wood, every tree is a buckler. When they fight in a plain, they fight with leaping and dancing that seldom an arrow hits, and when a man is wounded, they soon retire and save the wounded.[22]

It is and was an incredible misnomer to describe the Native Americans of New England as "savages", for there is little in the record to suggest that warfare was a way of life with them, and this for many complex reasons. The evidence is strong, based in the fact of a culture and civilization that appears to have prospered in the regions for thousands of years. Along with occasional disputes and rare cases of open

---

[21] Lescarbot, Marc, Les Muses de la Nouvelle France, Chez Jean Millot, (Paris, 1609) 43

warfare, other customary means of resolving arguments, disagreements and resentments included staging elaborate negotiating ceremonies, which sometimes resulted in high ranking marriage arrangements between sparring communities. However, probably the most ameliorating of all factors was the fecundity and complexity of the New England landscape, especially the fact that most Native American communities were separated by complex river systems extending to the coast. These natural barriers and abundance of food, of course, made it both difficult and unnecessary to mount large scale invasions over vast distances using canoes for transport, difficulties that were soon to be overcome once sailing ships and guns came into use by the Tarratines. Thus the balance of power was usurped and, in the process, traditional mores and customs were overthrown and made moot by the efficiency in killing provided by the technologies. Disputes and conflicts which had been managed successfully for years by bordering tribes were now subject to rapid resolution by the administration of brutalities never before witnessed by Native Americans in this region.

To understand how the Tarratines gained access to European technology and weapons, one is led to examine documents concerning Basque fishing off the coast of New England. Basque ships were observed and reported in large numbers by such early explorers as Jacque Cartier in 1535.[23] There is also some evidence that the Basques had been fishing the New England region as much as a century or more before Columbus. Basque ships and crews dominated the cod industry and had opened the doors as well to the fur trade, though the details are famously vague. Here, we are at an impasse, for most of these activities were undocumented, perhaps purposely in order to keep markets and fishing grounds secret. Questions and theories about pre-Columbian Basque voyages to North America have persisted and have been garnering intense interest in recent years, having been raised by such books as Mark Kurlansky's book, Cod, a Biography of the Fish that Changed the World. Kurlansky's treatise, though brief, reveals a treasure trove of previously ignored or misinterpreted historical data that reveals new information about Basque activities. He demonstrates that a robust

---

[22] Roger Williams, Key Into the Language of America, Sea Venture Press, (Boston, 1998) 31

[23] Burrage, Henry, Early English and French Voyages, 104

fishing industry along the Canadian coast was secretly conducted by the Basques as a means of avoiding tax impositions required by fishering off Iceland. He also maintains that the Basques never made any territorial claims in the region due to their reluctance to reveal to others their profitable discovery. Given this scenario, it suggests the possibility of trade and technology transfers very early indeed in New England.

Kurlansky argues that the main body of evidence for Basques in North America is found in the fact that Basque fisheries supplied much of Europe with Cod for centuries. Logistically, it can be argued that there is no better way to account for this success than if they had discovered America before Columbus. Why? The data and mathematics dictate that they would have required access to bays and islands in order to set up drying racks for the cod – places like Samoset's Monhegan Island. While one can only speculate on the extent of the relationship between early Basque fishermen and Native Americans, there is evidence that it involved the transmission of European technologies to the Tarratines in at least one recorded incident. It is found in ship records from a 1602 voyage by two English explorers named Captain Bartholomew Gosnold and Bartolomew Gilbert. Below is an excerpt from the ship log telling an amazing tale of an encounter with a small sailing vessel operated by Native American traders as they were rounding Cape Cod heading northeast to Maine. What makes this incident even more revealing is the lack of genuine surprise on the part of the English, almost as if such a possibility was expected. The encounter took place just off Cape Neddick on the southern coast of Maine:

> But on Friday the fourteenth of May, early in the morning, we made the land, being full of faire trees, the land somewhat low, certaine hummocks or hilles lying into the land, the shore ful of white sand, but very stony or rocky. And standing faire alongst by the shore about twelve of the clocke the same day, we came to an anker, where six Indians in a Baske-shallop with mast and saile, an iron grapple, and a kettle of copper, came boldly aboord us, one of them apparelled with a waistcoat and breeches of blacke sedge, made after our sea-fashion, hose and shoes on his feet; all the rest (saving one that had a paire of breeches

of blue cloth) were all naked. These people are of tall stature, broad and grim visage, of a blacke swart complexion, the eiebrowes painted white; their weapons are bowes and arrowes; it seemed by some words and signes they made, that some Basks of S. John de Luz, have fished or trade in this place, being in the latitude of 43 degrees.[24]

Most modern people would be surprised to learn that one of the first encounters between English explorers and Native Americans took place on the open ocean. Indeed, there may have been many more. But the evidence is clear. By the beginning of the 17th century, and perhaps many decades, if not centuries earlier, Native Americans of New England and Canada had already utilized European sailing craft for their own gain and possible military advantage. A dependency was formed as a result of the trade leading to the diminution of Native crafts and food production. It is well documented that robust trading activities were in place in the Atlantic Maritimes as early as 1535, attested to by the voyage of Jacque Cartier into the St. Lawrence. Much of the trade involved furs for guns, tools and other sundry items, but it would make logical sense that either Basques or French would have willingly constructed barques for trade to the Native Americans as well. Additional evidence for this technology transfer comes in a report of the voyage of Captain Popham, in 1607. In this case, the reporting is much more detailed than the Gosnald ship log, describing a significant trading encounter with French-aligned Tarratines along the coast of Nova Scotia near present-day Halifax harbor. In this case, not one, but two Tarratine shallops are encountered. If anything, it shows how profoundly Native American societies were being shaped by European influence far earlier than the Mayflower. Following are some excerpts from the ship's report of the encounter:

This island standeth in the latitude of 44d and 1/2 and hear we had nott ben att an anker past to howers beffore we espyed a bisken shallop cominge towards us havinge in her eyght Sallvages and a Lyttel salvage boye they cam near unto us and spoke unto us in

---

[24] Gardner, Frank A., *"The Story of the Planters ",* The American Historical Society Bulletin, vol. XVI no. 4, (Somerville, NJ 1922) p. 288

thear Language. and we makinge seignes to them that they should com abord us showinge unto them knyves glasses beads and throwinge into thear bott som bisket but for all this they wold nott com abord of us but makinge show to go from us, we suffered them. So when they wear a lyttell from us and seeing we proffered them no wronge of thear owne accord retorned and cam abord of us and three of them stayed all that nyght wit us the rest depted in the shallope to the shore makinge seignes unto us that they wold retorn unto us aggain the next daye. The next daye the same salvages with three salvage women beinge the fryst daye of August retorned unto us bringinge with them som fewo skines of bever in an other bisken shallop and properinge thear skines to trook with us but they demanded over muche for them and we seemed to make lyght of them. So then the other which had stayed with us all ngygt went into the shallop and so they depted. Ytt seem that the french hath trad with them for they use many french words. the Cheeff Comander of these people ys called Messamott and the ryver or harbor ys called emannett. we take these popell to be the tarentyns and thse peopell as we have learned sence do make wars with Sasanoa the Cheeffe Comander to the westward (Mawooshen)....[25]

To many, it might seem unfathomable that a seafaring Native American nation from Nova Scotia was prosecuting a war using European guns, swords, ships and other technology. However, given the evidence, it becomes transparently clear that English plans to colonize New England was the direct result of the two calamities, not just one – the epidemic of 1616-18 and the Tarratine War. Most historians have connected the settlement of New England with the much better documented event of the epidemic. But the more impending problem facing coastal Native Americans from Schoodic Bay south to Rhode Island were the French/Basque supplied and supported Tarratines, and

---

[25] Burrage, Henry S., <u>Early English and French Voyages</u>, (New York: Charles Scribner's Sons, 1932) p. 403

this as early as 1603, well before the epidemic. John Goff describes the impact of the hostilities, writing, "The Tarratine Wars, which raged fiercely in various stages all along the Atlantic coast from Nova Scotia, down the coast of Maine and to the tip of Cape Cod between 1603 and 1635, appear to have been a major and influential shaper of history, despite having been almost completely overlooked or ignored by historians."[26] This raises many questions. For instance, why is there no evidence for further hostilities on the Maine coast after around 1615, and why did the Tarratine invaders turn their attention south to Massachusetts by then? One might speculate that the undocumented arming of Mawooshen by English traders might have been a factor, along with the scattered presence of English fishing stations and trading posts sponsored by the profit-driven Gorges' company. Those factors together would suggest a context to the efforts of Samoset in Plimoth. He may merely have been attempting to extend an already strong alliance between the Gorges sponsored stations in Maine south into Massachusetts.

The most powerful sachem of the Massachusetts at the time of the epidemic was Nanapashemet, A Pawtucket (Massachusett) sachem. The Pawtuckets, based just north of Boston, were known for having dominion over the Massachusett tribe occupying the area snorth of the Charles River to the Merrimac River and west to Concord, with major villages in the Watertown, Salem, Lynn, Chelsea and Medford areas. Some historians claim that his influence spread south from the Merrimac River to Weymouth, and then west to the Connecticut River, thus including the inland Nipmucs. A year or two before the epidemic broke out, Nanapashemet led a large group of warriors to assist the Mawooshen-aligned Penobscots in a bloody battle against the Tarratines. Following the battle, he returned home only to witness his people ravaged by the epidemic in 1618, with as many as 90% in the Boston area losing their lives. Nanepashemit, himself, survived the epidemic due to having been barricaded against Tarratine attacks in a remote spot in Medford. But then tragedy struck again when the Tarratines, in 1619, mounted a revenge attack against him in which he lost his life. Surviving Nanepashemit was his wife, known only as Squaw Sachem, who

---

[26] Goff, John V., "Remembering the Tarratines and Nanepashemet", NEARA Journal, Vol. 39, number 2 (2009) 16

took up the mantle of her husbands leadership and rallied her people, perhaps 300-400 in number, compared to the estimated 3,000 or more living along the Charles River before the Tarratine War and epidemic. However, their survival was about to be even more sorely tested when waves of Puritan immigrants began surging into Boston in 1629.

The selective rendering of historical data has left behind many open questions regarding the early history of New England, some answerable, but most beyond the pale of our modern understanding. Most unfortunately, this is the case of the Tarratine War, an episode which forever changed New England in ways we still do not recognize, thus we are unable to fathom the true scope of it. So, instead of a dedicated ethnography, a fair and honest portrayal of Native Americans, students have been taught the negative myths adopted by Pilgrims and Puritans in the 17th century. Although we dress it up in Thanksgiving holiday garb, the devaluation of Native culture, economies and people resulted in the oppression of those communities, and eventually far greater sufferings to come. To most colonists, Native Americans and their stories, culture and concerns were not worthy of consideration nor honest representation in print, a trend which has continued into modern times.

Chapter Two
The Theology of Encroachment

The Puritans came to New England with the financial support and resources of the Massachusetts Bay Company. A patent authorizing the company to take possession of land around Massachusetts Bay was procured from the Plimoth (England) Council on March 19, 1628. That initial authorization was further confirmed the following year with the issuance of a Royal Charter giving the Company rights of governance within the bounds of the patent. By the end of the next decade, in 1640, over twenty thousand English settlers had filtered into the Massachusetts Bay and Plimoth colonies, and from there had spread out into Connecticut, Rhode Island, Maine and other distant places.

Having secured legal authority for settlement, the Puritans refocused their attention upon the religious mandate which undergirded their intentions for New England. There were many reasons behind the Puritan claims that their god had selected them for a divine mission in the wilderness and that it was also the divine will that they should appropriate another nation's land as their own. No person articulated this doctrine more forcefully nor enacted it more effectively than John Winthrop, elected Governor of the colony upon his arrival in 1630 on the Arabella. One of the immediate responsibilities of the new governor was to expedite the prompt appropriation and distribution of land to the shiploads of immigrants arriving on the colony's doorstep. Within five years, under Winthop's oversight, much of the Bay region was seized or purchased, mathematically divided acre by acre, and distributed under a township system which would then take on the responsibility of separate allotments. This policy was challenged at many levels by the Native Americans, but also by other adversaries, both in the colonies and England.

One of the most vigorous critics of Puritan policy was Roger Williams, who was banished from Massachusetts in 1634, partly because of his opposition to the Puritan justification of their seizure of Native American land. Williams insisted that all land must be purchased from the neighboring sachems and sagamores in accordance with tribal custom and universally accepted standards of justice. Williams' argument sought to invalidate the theological claims of the Puritans. In the end, Williams' protests were roundly and directly rejected by Winthrop, who countered with the preposterous notion that English confiscation of land would actually benefit the Native Americans. He wrote:

> That wch lies comon, & hath never beene replenished or subdued, is free to any that possesse & improve it: for God hath givven to the sonnes of men a double right to the earth; theire is a naturall right, & a civill right. ...As for the Natives in New England, they inclose noe Land, neither have any setled habytation, nor any tame Cattle to improve the Land by, & soe have no other but a Naturall Right to those Countries. Soe as if we leave them sufficient for their use, we may lawfully take the rest, there being more then enough for them & us.
>
> God hath consumed the Natives wth a great Plauge in those parts, soe as there be few Inhabitants lefte. It is the revealed will of God that the Gospel should be preached to all nations, & though we know not whether these Barbarians will receive it at first or noe, yet it is a good worke to serve Gods providence in offering it to them (& this is fittest to be doone by Gods owne servants) for God shall have glory by it though they refuse it, & there is good hope that the Posterity shall by this meanes be gathered into Christs sheepefould.[27]

The Puritans took their mission as one of exalted religious importance, believing that their success would inspire conversions to Christianity across the continent of America, often resorting to typological method to define themselves in relation to the Native Americans. The Puritans were Jews, and the Native Americans the heathen – Philis-

---

27 John Winthrop, "Diverese objections wch have been made against this Plantation, wth their answears & Resolutions," in <u>Life and Letters of John Winthrop</u>, 1588- 1630, Robert C. Winthrop, ed. (Boston: Ticknor and Fields 1864), 311-313.

tines, Canaanites, Moabites and the many other nations portrayed in the biblical literature. Of course, this typology would prove deadly to Native Americans, even as it provided Puritan visionaries such as John Cotton, Increase Mather, Edward Johnson and many others also to make sense of their collective European plight in New England. Others, such as John Eliot went further, suggesting that the conversion of heathen Native Americans would spark a world-wide conversion of Jews, which in turn would bring the "kingdom of God" to earth. Eliot's theories were based upon his belief that Native Americans represented the lost tribes of Israel, and that their conversion would spread to the land of biblical Israel. Over and over again, we see this eschatological note in the thinking of Puritans, a note that is still strong in the undercurrents of contemporary American religious life. Thus, many Americans, as much as any other nation, persist in their belief in America as a Christian nation pre-ordained for greatness. Unfortunately, that same conviction has left behind a questionable legacy in colonial New England, one which is so painful to behold that it has been submerged beneath the great mythologies of this nation's founding.

By the logic of Puritan typology, the occurrence of the great epidemic (1616-18) was accorded as divine intervention on behalf of the Puritan settlements. Nevertheless, while the epidemic had cleared their way by decimating New England, they were frightfully aware that their own settlements were but minuscule outposts in a land that was teeming with other Native American civilizations. The comparisons, of course, did not always match up with the realities of their situation, but metaphors are malleable, and a paradigm was constructed from the resulting falsehoods as a result. This was what proved to them that they were indeed the chosen people and that New England was the "New Canaan". Extending the logic even further, the epidemics which killed so many Native Americans found their biblical equivilant in the plagues sent by their god against the Egyptians in the story of the Exodus. By this measure, each success against the enemy seemed to signal divine approval, while each failure the punishment for their own sins and unfaithfulness. Thus, the coincidences between their perceived situation and the Biblical story of the Exodus were so exaggerated that it became ingrained in their consciousness as religious dogma.

Typology uses poetic and symbolic interpretation. Its use in

The Theology of Encroachment

Christianity originates in the New Testament, but also predates it as well. There is nothing mysterious about its use. Throughout Christian history, typology was often used as a methodology in Biblical interpretation. Using the tool, the scripture appears transparent, providing a ready key to understanding past history, the present and future. The legendary figures in Biblical history are read as antetypes, behind which one may perceive the form of future events. The method is based upon making comparisons, so it is a subjective science, colored by the needs and desires of the interpreter.

One does not have to read much Puritan theology without discovering some of the mistakes they made in interpreting their experiences in light of scripture. For an obvious example, the Puritans conceived of the New England landscape as a wilderness. Even today, a popular misconception of New England history is that the first European explorers encountered a vast wilderness. Of course, this is not true. What they did encounter was a vast civilization, thousands of years old, and made up of many cultures and religious heritages, certainly as many, and likely more than the rather homogenous societies of Europe. But these models, based on oral tradition, made little sense and had even less intrinsic positive meaning to the invaders upon their initial encounters. What the Puritans saw, instead of the ancient cultures occupying New England, was the opaque and obscure outlines of Biblical history transcribed mysteriously upon their situation in New England. To the Puritan, the Pequots might just as well be Moabites, and the Narragansetts, Philistines. The Puritans made few attempts to understand Native American civilizations and cultures, and instead imposed their own preconceived notions concerning native peoples according to typological categories. This typology also extended to the land, with many Puritan preachers using the metaphors found in the book of Exodus. This fantasy lent itself to the overall paradigm of "chosen people" asserting dominion over New England as a "New Canaan" – a divinely-appointed refuge for a divinely anointed people. Of course, this imagery assumed a retrogressive theology incapable of rational analysis, and a fatal impediment to a peaceful and respectful co-existence with Native Americans. Historian Peter Carrol analyzes some of the implications of their attitudes: "The Puritans had developed specific views of the wilderness situation prior to their migration to Massachusetts Bay.

...Furthermore, as the children of Israel, they translated their hardships in the New World as God's testing of his chosen people – a necessary prelude to everlasting salvation." [28]

The correspondences which suggested this typological understanding were vivid. The flight from persecutors and the dangerous journey across the formidable Atlantic Ocean was compared to Moses leading the people across the Red Sea in flight from the Egyptian forces. Of course, the implications are clear. The Puritans saw themselves as the new chosen people set aside for a divine mission in America. This interpretation in subsequent years provided an underlying rationale for everything from missionary activity to wars of conquest. The implications of this doctrine were disastrous for Native Americans throughout New England. Thus the "English Israel" was called to fulfill their god's plan, the fulfillment of which, from their view, would ultimately require either conversion, subjection, or destruction of the Native Americans and their culture. While conversion of the Native Americans was espoused (and widely advertised) as a first priority of the Puritan mission in New England, the Massachusetts Bay Company originally had made neither provision nor allocated resources to that end. The Puritans had an insidious, but hidden political agenda, whether that applied to Native Americans or non-conforming European settlers in the region. Winning new converts were secondary. Acquiring land was first priority for Puritans, and that process was hastened in 1637 with a genocidal attack by English forces that would virtually wipe out the Pequot tribe in Connecticut. Typology defined the Native American as an enemy, but it did not define an appropriate response. That was left for the ministers and theologians to decide, powers which few clergy anywhere in the world at that time could claim.

In 1628, the first major advance of Puritan settlers surged into the area known as Naumkeag (Salem), named after the people who lived there and took the name as their identity. Previously, a fishing station at Naumkeag had been operating under the leadership of Roger Conant, who had received accommodation from the local Naumkeag village for two years before unceremoniously being displaced by a group of

---

28 Peter N. Carroll, <u>Puritanism and the Wilderness,</u> (New York: Columbia University Press 1969), 2.

The Theology of Encroachment

Puritans led by John Endicott, first governor of New England. Judging from the decade long history of English fishing and trading activities, a relationship of equals was conferred in these arrangements with fishermen. The Puritan onrush was different, and we can little doubt that the Naumkeags were not ready for what would follow in the fishermen's stead. How did they accept English presence on their ancestral lands? Here is another area in which the answer is not clear, as there is little in the record to suggest anything other than acquiescence. Throughout this historical period, the lack of native perspective requires assumptions to be made, but here we are on safe grounds. The sheer numbers on the English side would have settled any possible resistance in Naumkeag or anywhere else in Massachusetts as well.

It has been estimated that in pre-contact times there were at least twelve Massachusetts village sites along the Charles River alone. As a result, land that had been formerly cultivated by the native inhabitants was abundant, and within two years settlers established hundreds of farms and founded the towns of Boston, Roxbury, Cambridge, Charlestown, and Dorchester on formerly settled sites. By 1630, most of the Massachusetts Native Americans around the northern part of the bay were concentrated in areas just north of Boston, many under the leadership of the Squaw Sachem. Puritan communities were rapidly springing to life throughout the region between 1630-1634, with the towns of Naumkeag (Salem) and Boston serving as the hubs for outlying settlements. New towns such as Ipswich, Newbury, and Rowley were rapidly formed along the coast, as well as inland communities such as Andover and Woburn.

The Puritans spared no expense to insure that these rapidly expanding towns would be armed from the start. As a precondition for settlement rights, the colonists were expected to share in the cost of armaments and common defense. Forts were erected and cannons were posted in strategic locations. A common store of ordinance was required, and a militia was recruited in each community. Professional soldiers had also been recruited from the start, along with specialized craftsmen to help construct and maintain fortifications. Most importantly, individual colonists were urged and required to own and bear arms themselves. Edward Johnson's solemn admonitions to the "forerunners of Christ's army" to fully arm themselves is reflected more concretely in Company records. The following excerpt is a suggested list of necessary items to supply an average of one hundred men, and demonstrates the high priority placed on military preparedness:

> 3 drums, to each two pair of heads,
> 2 ensigns,
> 2 partisans fo captain and leftenant,
> 3 halberds, for three sergeants,
> 80 bastard muskets, with snaphances, four foot in the barrel, without rests,
> 6 long fowling-pieces, with musket bore, six and a half foot long,
> 10 full muskets, four foot barrel, with matchcoocks and rests,
> 90 bandoleers, for the muskets, each with a bullet bag,
> 10 horn flasks, for the long fowling-pieces, to hold two pound apiece, and
> 100 swords, and belts,
> 60 corselets, and 60 pikes, 20 half pikes,
> 12 barrels powder
> Shot, 1 lb. to a bandoleer,
> 8 pieces of land ordnance for the fort, whereof 5 already provided [29]

The arms buildup was totally incommensurate with the potential threat which local Native American villagers may have posed to the new immigrants. The horrendous effects of repeated epidemics decimated the already weakened villages to the point that any opposition to English encroachment from the Massachusetts tribe was no longer feasible. There was also a sense of divine intervention in the tragedy. An official transcript of the sorrowful event survives in the Charlestown Records. Despite the sorrowfulness, however, even this relatively sympathetic recorder could not prevent himself from interpreting the impact of the epidemics upon the Native American population to the

---

[29] "Records of the Governor and Company of the Massachusetts Bay in New England", in <u>Chronicles of the First Planters of the Colony of Massachusetts Bay From 1623-1636</u>, Alexander Young, ed. (Boston: Charles C. Little and James Brown 1846), 43-45.

The Theology of Encroachment

benevolence and favor of the Puritan god toward the English:

> At this time began a most grievous and terrible sickness amongst the Indians, who were exceeding numerous about us, (called the Aberginians.) The disease was generally the small pox, which raged not only amongst these, but amongst the Eastern Indians also, and in a few months swept away multitudes of them, young and old. They could not bury their dead; the English were constrained to help; and that which is very remarkable is, that though the English did frequently visit them in their sickness, notwithstanding the infection, it was observed that not one Englishman was touched with the disease. But it was extremely infectious among themselves, and mortal where it took any of them; insomuch as there was scarce any of them left. By which awful and admirable dispensation it pleased God to make room for his people of the English nation; who, after this, in the immediate years following, came from England by many hundreds every year to us, who, without this remarkable and terrible stroke of God upon the natives, would with much more difficulty have found room, and at far greater charge have obtained and purchased land.[30]

The experience and attitudes of the Massachusetts Bay Company somewhat paralleled that of Plimoth with regard to Native American relations. As most Puritan testimony shows, the Massachusetts welcomed their presence in their territory. One settler at Salem is recorded describing relations with neighboring Native Americans, "They do generally profess to like well of our coming and planting here; partly because there is abundance of ground that they cannot possess nor make use of, and partly because our being here will be a means of both relief to them when they want, and also a defence from the enemies, wherewith before this Plantation began, they were often

---

[30]"The Charlestown Records, Chapter XIX (1633)" in <u>Chronicles of the First Planters of the Colony of Massachusetts Bay From 1623-1636</u> (Boston: Charles C. Little and James Brown 1846), 386-387.

endangered."[31]

Of course, Massachusett Native Americans were not relieved to find others take control of their territory, and instead of providing protection from enemies, the English presence was far more threatening to them in the end. The rapidly shrinking Native American population hastened the process of capitulation as sagamores beat a path to Boston in deference to their new overlords. Gov. Winthrop, seizing the opportunity, quickly established diplomatic relationships with area sagamores who had previously been reluctant to welcome English settlements. His efforts were rewarded with success even with Chickatabot, whose men had been brutally massacred, and his mother's gravesite defaced by Plimoth settlers. Of course, it must also be recognized that fear of further atrocities was a major motivator in getting Native Americans to submit. Winthrop described his first encounter with Chickatabot:

> Chickatabot came with his sannops and squaws, and presented the governor with a hogshead of Native American corn. After they had all dined, and had each a small cup of sack and beer, and the men tobacco, he sent away all his men and women, (though the governor would have stayed, in regard of the rain and thunder). Himself and one squaw and one sannop stayed all night, and, being in English clothes, the governor set him at his own table, where he behaved himself as soberly, etc., as an Englishman.[32]

The possibility for trade was another important reason for Massachusetts Native Americans to submit to English authority, with Native Americans' desire and intentions to gain access to weapons at the forefront. But that only happened because there were people like Thomas Morton who were willing to flout the restrictions which Pilgrim and Puritan alike imposed against Native Americans. In fact, that kind of trade was snuffed out with the ouster of Thomas Morton. In the end, trading was the most dangerous activity of all for Native Americans.

---

31 Francis Higginson, "New-England Plantation" (1630), in <u>Chronicles of the First Planters of the Colony of Massachusetts Bay from 1623-1636</u>, 257.

32 John Winthrop, <u>Winthrop's Journal 1630-1649</u>, vol. I (New York: Charles Scribner's Sons, 1908), 59.

Besides undermining traditional economies and technologies, European trade goods and settlers were accompanied by a whole new host of diseases such as flu, measles, smallpox and many others to which native Americans had no natural resistance. While the great epidemic of 1616-18 resulted in a multitude of deaths, most occurred along the Massachusetts and Maine coast, sparing such groups as the Narragansetts, Pequots and Mohegans. But once Puritan settlers began to pour in by the thousands, infiltrating the interior portions of New England, the problems were compounded as a host of various, many undiagnosed diseases wreaked havoc on new populations. Common diseases such as the flu were completely new to America, and that which brought a few days of misery to a European often brought death to Native Americans. In addition to disease, further devastation was caused by the introduction of rats during early contact period. Rats, besides for harboring the deadly bubonic plague, were destructive to native food storage caches, being able to burrow far deeper than native rodents and invade the winter stockpiles. While corn supplies had functioned as a kind of insurance against late winter starvation, this vital vestige of Native American technology was soon rendered useless by rats. Thus, as one economy and its technologies and social supports disintegrated, another more lethal to Native Americans and their interests emerged, a cash economy based on competition rather than cooperation.

The trade patterns, and not just the trade goods, which had been introduced by English, Dutch and French agents in the region created a relationship of mutual dependency between the two cultures, one mainly dependent upon credit and debts. This was particularly true of New England, where mutual advantages gained in the trade of land for English trade goods seemed to ameliorate the drawbacks of English neighbors in the Algonquin imagination. Indeed, if it had not been for the willingness of Algonquin tribes to sell their excess corn to the first beleaguered settlements, it is unlikely that any of them would have survived. But reciprocity involves more than one set of intentions, and the initial generosity and trust of the Algonquin toward the English settlers had tragic consequences for them as the expansionist English used it to their own exclusive advantage. This was particularly true in the case of guns.

Without guns, it was inevitable that the initial reciprocity in the trading relationship was soon to fall to the Native Americans further economic disadvantage. When the supply of furs, game, and excess lands began to dwindle, and as English farms and domesticated livestock began to supply most of the colony's food needs, the Massachusetts found themselves in a precarious economic position. Furthermore, in a variety of different types of transactions, particularly land, the English used various means from outright lies to threats in order to gain advantages. If an Native American was unhappy with the prices offered by a local English trader, it was a long overland trek to Hartford or Albany just to sell a few furs. Furthermore, increased trapping, due to the commercialization of these enterprises, led to the depletion of beaver and other fur bearing animals. With little to trade, and their neolithic crafts and pottery traditions quickly being lost due to disuse, the position of the Native Americans as trading partners with the English was undermined, and their material security threatened. In addition, as the Puritan colony expanded, other economic and social pressures on Native American villages increased. One of the most serious was the constant damage to Massachusetts agriculture by English cattle and pigs, making even subsistence farming impractical without elaborate fences. This pattern was duplicated throughout New England whenever English farms encroached upon Native American land, and Native American crops ended as fodder for Puritan animals destined for Puritan stomachs.

One of the prominent aspects of Puritan land acquisition was the use of a double standard in regard to English and Native Americans. One germane example of this attitude is the change in Puritan policies toward the selling and disposal of lands once held in English title, which mandated that Massachusetts Native American territorial claims and land use customs be held in abeyance while the Puritans quickly seized or bought whatever they could. It was a simple and duplicitous action. Once bought, those same lands were put into a completely different legal status which conferred permanent control to the individual town governments. In practice, this policy violated every norm of civilized behavior and English law and owed its origins to typological method. Below are several sections from the law providing an insight into Puritan thinking:

> First, Forasmuch as the right of disposals of the

Inheritance of all Lands in the Countrey, lyeth in the General Court, whatsoever Lands are given and assigned by the General Court, to any Town or person shall belong and remain as right of Inheritance to such Townes and their successors, and to such persons and to the heires and Assignes as their propiety for ever.

As God in old time, in the Common-wealth of Israell, forbad the alienation of Lands from one Tribe to another, so to prevent the like incovenience in the alienation of Lands, from one Towne to another it were requisite to be ordered.

1. First, that no free Burgesse, or free Inhabitant of any Town shall sell the Land alloted to him in the Towne, (unlesse the free Burgesse of the Towne give consent unto such sale, or refuse to give due price answerable to what other offer without fraud) but to some one or other of the free Burgesses, or free inhabitants of the same Towne.[33]

The permanent alienation of formerly Native American-owned territory was a signal to Native Americans that their status was that of an inferior people, and that they had been relegated to a marginal existence as exiles within their own homeland. For the Massachusetts Native Americans in 1634, resistance must have seemed futile, for they neither had the numbers nor the influence to gain leverage in any matter of importance to them. On the other hand, the fact that the Massachusetts Native Americans represented a rather benign foe for the Puritan allowed for some assimilation of Native Americans into the general economy of the English. Records show that many were quick to learn and make use of European technology and adapt to European ways. But the effects were minimal, mainly because of religious and cultural prejudices fostered by Puritan typology. In particular, Massachusett spiritual beliefs and practices were held in great disdain and harshly condemned by comparing them to witchcraft. Furthermore,

---

33 John Cotton, "An Abstract of the Lawes of New England" in The New England Way, (New York:AMS Press, Inc., 1984), 8.

this abhorrence and intolerance for native culture was expressed at the government level through demands for conformity to English practices, establishing a pattern of cultural genocide that, in time, spread and repeated itself from New England westward to the Pacific.

In other ways, Native Americans were subjected to Puritan policy for more devious purposes. For instance, the Puritans allowed that Native Americans living within the jurisdiction of the Massachusetts Bay government were required to live within the bounds of the civil laws of the colony, and be subject to the same penalties as the English for infractions. The critical difference is that the Puritans administered their judgments through the various sachems and councils in Massachusetts villages, putting sachems in the uncomfortable position of punishing his people for their violations of Puritan customs and laws, a lamentable reminder of the shift in power relationships which took place with Puritan occupation. John Winthrop narrates an example of the practice:

> At a court not long before, two of Chickatabott's men were convented and convicted for assaulting some English of Dorchester in their houses, etc. they were put in the biboes, and Chickatabot required to beat them, which he did.[34]

With the Massachusetts rendered both militarily and legally powerless to resist both encroachment and efforts to destroy their culture and way of life, Puritan leaders turned their attention elsewhere. Indeed, even before the major immigration of the 1630's, the Massachusetts Company had set down priorities for their first settlement under Governor Endicott in Naumkeag (Salem). These had little to do with the Massachusett Native Americans, and much to do with other European competition, including other English! This is reflected quite explicitly in the Company's list of instructions for Endicott, containing little more than a note of concern for public relations regarding the Native Americans: "If any of the salvages pretend right of inheritance to all or any part of the lands granted in our patent, we pray you endeavor to purchase their titles, that we may avoid the least scruple of intrusion."[35] Of course, much of the land was quickly appropriated since

---

[34] Winthrop, <u>Winthrop's Journal</u> (vol. 1), 89.

The Theology of Encroachment

few Native Americans were present to raise serious objections, and although the gravity of what was happening may not have dawned on the participants, other English competitors were keenly aware of it and determined to stop the Puritan progress in its tracks. The most significant competitor of the Puritan movement was Sir Ferdinando Gorges and his powerful associates through the Plimoth Company. By 1629, Gorges' agents were being unceremoniously evicted from lands around the bay by zealous Puritans, bolstered by legal contrivances without underlying authority. This reflected both the Puritan presumption of power along with a strategy which would procure and guarantee their sovereignty in New England. Below is a sample of a legal contrivance:

> I find Mr. Oldham's grant from Mr. Gorge is to him and John Dorrell, for all the lands within Mattachusetts Bay, between Charles river and Abousett river, containing in length, by a straight line, five miles up the said Charles river, into the main land northwest from the border of the said Bay, including all creeks and points by the way, and three miles in length from the mouth of the foresaid river of Abousett, up into the main land, upon a straight line southwest, including all creeks and points, and all the land in breadth and length between the foresaid rivers, with all prerogatives, royal mines excepted. The rent reserved is twelve pence on every hundred acres of land that shall be used; William Blaxton, clerk, and William Jeffryes, gentleman, authorized to put John Oldham in possession. Having a sight of his grant, this I found. Though I hold it void in law, yet his claim being to this, you may, in your discretion, prevent him by causing some to take possession of the chief part thereof.[36]

By 1630, the first wave of Puritan immigrants was large enough to work to their overwhelming advantage, and they rapidly consolidated

---

[35] "The Company's First General Letter of Instructions to Endicott and His Council (In Gravesend, the 17th of April, 1629)", in <u>Chronicles of the First Planters of the Colony of Massachusetts Bay From 1623-1636, 159.</u>

[36] Ibid., 169.

power. A new government in Boston, under the governorship of John Winthrop, did make accommodations to non-Puritans when necessary out of political concern, such as granting limited trading privileges and continued occupancy on formerly Native American owned lands. But enactment of new governing powers virtually excluded dissenting voices within the new communities under the penalty of death. There was no question about who was in control. Nevertheless, this was a difficult policy to maintain as the Puritans had to walk a thin line between abrogating English legal tradition and maintaining the principles of their religious commonwealth.

As a result, many other English settlers, Puritan and non-Puritan alike, felt that the Massachusetts Bay Company had crossed the line in asserting their authority and imposing laws prejudicial to religious non-conformists. By 1634, the abuse of this power had already caused Roger Williams and a trickle of non-conformists to flee to the welcoming shelter of the Narragansetts in Rhode Island. Roger Williams, in particular, would become the bane of Massachusetts Bay Company as he challenged the Puritan government on a host of issues. One in particular, was the issue of the patent, which the Puritans maintained gave them the right to seize the lands formerly claimed by Native American tribes. While Williams is often celebrated for his efforts on behalf of religious liberty, he was just as vociferous, and perhaps even more dangerous to Puritan interests in his opposition to Puritan assertions of "vacuum domocilum" as the basis for confiscation of Native American land. The Puritan colony was quick to react to Williams' charges, particularly John Cotton, asserting the Puritan prerogative to establish a Mosaic Commonwealth in Massachusetts. Following is a section from his written response, "To Return the Patent Back Again to the King":

> By the patent it is, that we [the settlers of Massachusetts Bay] received allowance from the King to depart his kingdom, and to carry our goods with us, without offense to his officers, and without paying custom to himself. By the patent, certain select men as magistrates, and freemen) have power to make laws, and the magistrates to execute justice, and judgment amongst the people, according to such laws.
>
> By the patent we have power to erect such a gov-

ernment of the church, as is most agreeable to the Word, to the estate of the people, and to the gaining of natives (in God's time) first to civility, and then to Christianity. To this authority established by this patent, Englishmen do readily submit themselves: and foreign plantations (the French, the Dutch, and Swedish) do willingly transact their negotiations with us, as with a colony established by the royal authority of the state of England.

This patent, Mr. Williams publicly, and vehemently preached against, as containing matter of falsehood, and injustice: falsehood in making the King the first Christian prince who had discovered these parts: and injustice, in giving the country to his English subjects, which belonged to the native Indians. This therefore he pressed upon the magistrates and people, to be humbled for from time to time in days of solemn humiliation, and to return the patent back again to the King. It was answered to him, first, that it was neither the King's intendment, nor the English planters' to take possession of the country by murder of the natives, or by robbery; but either to take possession of the void places of the country by the law of nature, (for vacuum domicilium cedit occupanti:) or if we took any lands from the natives, it was by way of purchase, and free consent. A little before our coming, God had by pestilence, and other contagious diseases, swept away many thousands of the natives, who had inhabited the Bay of Massachusetts, for which the patent was granted. Such few of them as survived were glad of the coming of the English, who might preserve them from the oppression of the Narragansetts. For it is the manner of the natives, the stronger nations to oppress the weaker. This answer did not satisfy Mr. Williams, who pleaded, the natives, though they did not, nor could subdue the country, (but left it vacuum domicilium) yet they hunted all the country over, and for the expedition of their hunting voyages, they burnt up all the underwoods in the country, once or twice a year, and therefore as noble men in England possessed great parks, and the King great forests in England only for their game, and no man might lawfully invade their propriety, so might the natives challenge the like propriety of the country here. It was replied unto him

1. That the King, and noble men in England, as they possessed greater territories than other men, so they did greater service to church, and commonwealth.
2. That they employed their parks, and forests, not for hunting only, but for timber, and for the nourishment of tame beasts, as well as wild, and also for habitation to sundry tenants.

That our towns here did not disturb the huntings of the natives, but did rather keep their game fitter for their taking; for they take their deer by traps, and not by hounds.

4. That if they complained of any straits we put upon them, we gave satisfaction in some payments, or other, to their content.

We did not conceive that it is a just title to so vast a continent to make no other improvement of millions of acres in it, but only to burn it up for pastime. But these answers not satisfying him, this was still pressed by him as a national sin, to hold to the patent, yea, and a national duty to renounce the patent: which to have done, had subverted the fundamental state and government of the country.[37]

The interpretation of the patent and the authority which Puritans assumed from it was devastating to the Native Americans. It must also be emphasized that, by 1640, Rhode Island was a hotbed of dissent, its growing towns filled with Baptists, Quakers, secularists, and

---

37 John Cotton, "To Return the Patent Back Again to the King, in Puritans, Indians and Manifest Destiny, Charles M. Segal and David C. Stineback, ed. (New York: G,P. Putnam's Sons, 1977), 80-81.

other non-conformists. Many, such as Anne Hutchinson and some of her followers, had settled there as a result of banishment, while others emigrated out of the Puritan colony voluntarily. With the approval of the Narragansetts, the English population quickly expanded, providing a hedge of deterrence which gave protection to the Narragansett nation as well as the new settlers themselves. Obviously, the proximity of this community of non-conformists and Native Americans threatened Massachusetts Bay. As a result, the Puritan government began to suspect the Narragansetts for many reasons, but most importantly, they perceived the pact between them and the new settlements as an affront and a challenge to Puritan pre-eminence in the region.

Chapter Three
The Pequot Massacres

> The number they thus destroyed, was conceived to be above Four hundred. At this time it was a fearful sight to see them frying in the Fire, and the streams of Blood quenching the same; and horrible was the stink and scent thereof: but the Victory seemed a sweet Sacrifice, and they gave the praise thereof to God, who had wrought so wonderfully for them, thus to enclose their enemies in their hands, and given them so speedy a Victory over so proud, insulting, and blasphemous an Enemy. [38]

By 1633, the Puritans had subdued the Massachusetts and their allies, and settled across the Massachusetts Bay area. As new settlers continued to arrive, the availability of vacant land in the region declined, and soon there was a growing clamor among the new immigrants for more. Even John Winthrop himself was cognizant of the impracticality of accommodating the stream of new immigrants in the bay area. In a letter to Sir Simon D'Ewes in England, Winthrop discussed the difficulties facing the new government, claiming that all surplus lands in the bay area had already been apportioned.[39] The implications of this scarcity can hardly be understated. The pressure to grow enough food was but one problem. The most urgent one, however, was the growing dissent among new arrivals wanting land. But, in 1633, southern New England was still populated with powerful Native American tribes, particularly the Pequots and Narragansetts, neither of which had been affected by the great epidemic in 1616-18. Together, the Narragansetts and Pequots represented the biggest obstacle to Puritan ambitions. In addition, the Dutch had already established themselves at Manhattan and Albany and, in 1632, established a trading post on the present day site of Hartford along the western side of the Connecticut river. The Massachusetts Bay Colony was not the only

---

[38] Nathaniel Morton, New England's Memorial, (Boston: The Club of Odd Volumes, 1903), 101.
[39] Neal Salisbury, Manitou and Providence, (New York: Oxford University Press, 1982), 192.

The Pequot Massacres

English group with ambitions for the region.

Edward Winslow, in 1631, at the invitation of sachems from the local Tunxis, Podunk, Sicaog and Poquonock tribes, visited the Connecticut River. The local tribes, like the Massachusetts and others, perceived an English presence as a hedge against incursions by the powerful Iroquois to the west and the Pequots to the south. By 1633, a group from Plimoth, led by a military officer, Lieut. William Holmes, set up a stockaded settlement and trading post just a few miles north of the Dutch trading post at Hartford, stirring a dispute between the rivals. Further complicating the arrangement, a royal charter had also been issued to other Puritan interests under the sponsorship of the Lords Say and Brooke and the Saybrook Company for settlement of the harbor and lands around present day New London, though the Dutch had also posted a small settlement at the mouth of the Connecticut River. Of course, this was Pequot and Eastern Niantic territory, although Native American claims were never seriously considered by the English company; in the end, it would be conquest, not deeds or purchases that would realize English goals for the region.

With all of the aforementioned in the background, the legal minds in Boston realized early that a way of breaching the legal parameters would be necessary in order to occupy Connecticut. Because of this legal impediment, Plimoth, while not even holding a patent for lands they already occupied, eventually declined to enter the high stakes gambit involved in colonization beyond their borders. As a result Plimoth remained satisfied with maintaining the lone trading post. But the lack of a legal mandate or patent did little to discourage the other settlers seated to the north on Massachusetts Bay.

As disputes and diplomatic wrangling between English, Dutch and Native Americans over territory in Connecticut continued to fester, a new threat to stability emerged with a splinter group of Puritans recently landed in Massachusetts. The land rush was on. Before Massachusetts Bay officials could initiate a strategy to establish a presence in Connecticut, the settlers grew impatient and were ready to move independently of Massachusetts Bay. One of their leaders was an influential Puritan minister named Thomas Hooker, pastor of a Cambridge congregation. Hooker's people were discouraged about the unavailability of land in the Massachusetts Bay region. Perhaps just as importantly,

Hooker's people were in disagreement with the strict policies regarding church membership and political rights.

In one fell swoop, however, the entire situation in Coonecticut changed when Dutch traders unknowingly unleashed two epidemics upon the native population. The first was evidently a smallpox epidemic which decimated the population around present-day Springfield, and the second was bubonic plague, which took a heavy toll southward, though sparing the relatively isolated Pequots in southern Connecticut. Although estimates vary, it is generally speculated that the two diseases killed as many as three fourths of the population in less than a year. Once again, disease cleared the way, further bolstering the Puritan inner conviction that their god had actually acted in their behalf, a belief enhanced by the fact that Europeans largely remained unscathed by diseases mortal to Native Americans. With renewed vigor, Puritan efforts were quickly multiplied with plans and preparations for military conquest moving forward, a fact that did not go unnoticed by the Pequots. On November 6, 1634, two Pequot ambassadors arrived in Boston with offers of friendship and a desire to negotiate a treaty with the colony. Winthrop and the majority of the General Court, however, were opposed to make any commitments to the Pequots, though a record of the negotiations shows that the Pequots were forthright about their motives and even obsequious in their generous offer. Winthrop describes the session:

> The reason why they desired so much our friendship was, because they were now in war with the Naragansetts, whom, till this year, they had kept under, and likewise with the Dutch who had killed their old sachem and some other of their men, wch for the Pekods had killed some Native Americans, who came to trade with the Dutch at Connecticut; and, by these occassions, they could not trade safely any where. Therefore they desired us to send a pinnace with cloth, and we should have all their trade. They offered us also all their right at Connecticut, and to further

---

[40] John Winthrop, "John Winthrop's Journal ", vol. 1, in <u>Original Narratives of Early American History</u>, James Kendal Hosmer, ed. (New York Charles Scribner' s Sons,1908) ,139

The Pequot Massacres

us what they could, if we would settle a plantation there.[40]

The Massachusetts Bay government was looking for much more than the trading partnership Pequots were willing to offer, in particular, exclusive dominance over vast new settlements in the fertile valleys and sheltered harbors of Pequot country. The negotiations were fruitless. To complicate matters even more, the Narragansetts had heard of the negotiations, and were fearful of an English and Pequot alliance. Tensions developed between the two tribes in 1633, when the Narragansetts were stricken with a smallpox epidemic which caused several thousand deaths. Taking advantage of the situation, a small group of Pequots took advantage of the Narragansetts' weakness and conducted raiding parties against them. The Narragansetts, therefore, were in no mood to tolerate the Pequots dalliances with the Puritan government. Winthrop relates an interesting sideline to the story about the Pequot ambassadors, writing, "The next morning, news came that two or three hundred of the Naragansetts were come to Cohann, viz. Neponsett, to kill the pekod ambassadors, etc. Presently we met at Roxbury, and raised some few men in arms, and sent to the Narragansett men to come to us."[41]

The meeting described above with the Narragansetts turned out to be less than anticipated, and was resolved without violence. In fact, it turned out to be somewhat of an exaggerated report, as only a small group of Narragansetts were discovered, and they disclaimed the report. Nevertheless, the situation posed another conundrum to the Massachusetts Bay government in the matter of the Pequots, namely the danger of a spinoff war with the powerful Narragansetts on their border. A delay was needed. The colony was still too unprepared to risk war with more than one tribe, and determined not to let the situation to spin out of control. We see this change of tactics reflected in a letter of Governor Winthrop to his son, John Winthrop, Jr., who was in England at the time:

> The Pekods sent two embassies to us. The first time, they went away without answer. The next time, we agreed a peace with them, (for friendly commerce only,) which was that they desired, having now war

---

[41] Ibid., 40.

> with the Dutch and Narigansetts, upon these terms, viz., that they should deliver us those men, who killed Capt. Stone, etc., and surrender up to us their right in Conecticott, which they willingly agreed unto, and offered us a great present of wampompeag, and beavers, and otter, with this expression, that we might, with part thereof, procure their peace with the Narigansetts, (themselves standing upon terms of honor, not to offer any thing of themselves).[42]

Here we find father and son involved in machinations and plots against the Pequots. Captain John Stone was an acknowledged slave trader who had previously murdered Native Americans, and asking them to be accountable for his death was beyond the pale. Both Winthrops knew this. Instead of delay, the effort only succeeded in heightening tensions, and the treaty was never ratified by Sassacus or the other sachems of the Pequots, notwithstanding Winthrop's pretense that there was an agreement. Thus, it is one of those suspicious accidents of history that no copy nor report of the treaty survived.

Whether or not there was a treaty with the Pequots, the illusion of a treaty gave the Puritans a somewhat tenuous legal rationale to establish their presence in Connecticut. The tenuous aspect was the demand that the killers of Captain John Stone be returned to Massachusetts in order to be punished. This appears to have been a totally disingenuous gesture. Stone had earned a reputation as a pirate and villain at Plimoth and Massachusetts Bay, and the Puritans had no legitimate reason to use him as a stumbling block in their relations with the Pequots. In fact, Stone had already been sentenced to death by the Plimoth authorities for attempting to hijack one of their vessels. But before the execution order could be administered, Stone escaped to the Massachusetts Bay colony, where he again elicited the wrath of authorities when he was caught in an act of adultery. Proceeding to verbally abuse the magistrates who were to try him, Stone then fled that colony in his vessel to sail to Virginia. On the way, he sailed up the Connecticut River where he and his men allegedly kidnapped some Native Americans, but were

---

[42] Robert C. Winthrop, ed., <u>Life and Letters of John Winthrop 1588-1630,</u> (Boston: Tecknor and Fields 1864), 125-126.

later discovered by Western Niantics who allegedly exacted revenge by killing him. So it would seem that both the Puritans and the Pequots had a reason to put the affair to rest. But the Puritan leaders instead took the issue of Stone to give them some leverage against the Pequots, namely, a reason to question their honor and extract more demands if they did not comply with the condition. A contemporary description of the infamous Captain Stone by Captain Roger Clapp demonstrates the duplicity of the Puritans' demands:

> There was also one Capt. Stone about the Year 1633 or 1634, who carried himself very proudly, and spake contemptuously of our Magistrates, and carried it lewdly in his Conversation. For his Misdemeanor, his Ship was stayed, but he fled and would not obey Authority: and there came Warrants to Dorchester to take him dead or alive; so all our Souldiers were in Arms, and Centinals were set in divers Places; and at length he was found in a great Corn-Field, where we took him and carried him to Boston; but for want of one Witness, when he came to his Trial, he escaped with his Life. He was said to be a Man of great Relation, and had great Favour in England; and he gave out threatning Speeches. Tho' he escaped with his Life, not being hanged for Adultery, there being but one Witness; yet for other Crimes he was fined, and payed it: And being dismissed he went towards Virginia; but by the way putting into the Pequot country to Trade with them, the Pequots cut off both him and his Men, took his Goods and burnt his Ship. Some of the Native Americans reported, That they Roasted him alive. Thus did God destroy him that so proudly threatened to ruin us by complaining against us when he came to England: Thus God destroyed him; and delivered us at that Time also. [43]

---

[43] Roger Clap, "Memoirs, &c.", in <u>Puritan Personal Writings: Autobiographies and Other Writings</u>, Sacvan Bercovitch, ed. (New York: AMS Press, Inc., 1989), 21.

Hidden Genocide, Hidden People

While Gov. Winthrop was trying to settle things between the Pequots and Narragansetts, he was also engaged in the struggle with Thomas Hooker and his plan to emigrate to Connecticut with his congregation. Winthrop's pretense of an agreement with the Pequots was clearly an attempt to disrupt the emigration plans. This was a period of high immigration and the number of dissatisfied settlers was growing rapidly. Francis Jennings outlines the meaning and impact of the agreement on the power struggle within the colony. He writes, "The Pequot treaty of 1634 had provided means for these astute gentlemen to extend their cooperating powers into the Connecticut Valley before Hooker even got there. The treaty had occurred during the period when the elder Winthrop and his supporters were attempting to dissuade Hooker's people from removing to Connecticut." [44]

Winthrop was playing two ends against the middle in all these negotiations. Winthrop also had a second 'card up his sleeve' through his son John Winthrop Jr. and his influence in England with Lord Say and Lord Brooke (the Saybrook Company). The Saybrook Company had received a charter to plant a colony in Connecticut, but had not yet implemented a plan. Winthrop conceived a plan through a deal with the Saybrook Company in order to gain legal control over the territory. The plan which was finally approved was for his son John Jr., in England at the time, to take control as Governor General of the territory, with the first step being the construction of a fort at the mouth of the Connecticut River under the dual authority of the Company and Massachusetts Bay. In this way, the Massachusetts Bay patent would be thus extended into the area where Hooker's contingent intended to settle. The plan was quickly implemented in 1635, with Winthrop Jr. sailing to Connecticut with soldiers, armaments, provisions, builders, and a generous financial stake, and enough men to build and supply the planned garrison. Once built, it was left under the command of Captain Lion Gardener, as Winthrop returned back to Massachusetts.

The report of a treaty with the Pequots alarmed many within Massachusetts Bay for other reasons too. One of the dissenters was the new pastor at Roxbury, John Eliot, soon to become famous for his mission efforts among the Native Americans. Eliot, probably with conversion of Native Americans rather than warfare with them in mind, had spo-

---

[44] Jennings, <u>Cant of Conquest</u>, 197.

The Pequot Massacres

ken out forcefully in a sermon against the plan, wary of its implications. But the Massachusetts Bay government was not prone to allowing this kind of dissenting opinion, and Eliot was quickly rebuked and censured by the leaders in Boston. Winthrop's duplicitous notes on the affair demonstrate the effectiveness of Puritan censors:

> It was informed us, how Mr. Eliot, the teacher of the church of Roxbury, had taken occasion, in a sermon, to speak of the peace made with the Pekods, and to lay some blame upon the ministry for proceeding therein, without consent of the people, and for other failings, (as he conceived). We took order, that he should be dealt with by Mr. Cotton, Mr. Hooker, and Mr. Welde, to be brought to see his error, and to heal it by some public explanation of his meaning; for the people began to take ocasion to murmur against us for it.
>
> It was likewise informed that Mr. Williams of Salem had broken his promise to us, in teaching publickly against the king's patent, and our great sin in claiming right thereby to this country, etc., and for usual terming the churches of England anti-Christian. We granted summons to him for his appearance at the next court.
>
> The aforesaid three ministers, upon conference with the said Mr. Eliot, brought him to acknowledge his error in that he had mistake the ground of his doctrine, and that he did acknowledge, that, for a peace only, (whereby the people were not to be engaged in a war,) the magistrates might conclude, plebe inconsulto, and so promised to express himself in public next Lord's day.[45]

The censure of Eliot was only the tip of the iceberg. While negotiations over the Pequots and the proposed settlement continued, the colony was also beset with growing internal dissent over theological matters. A strong antinomian* movement spearheaded by Anne

---

45 Winthrop, Winthrop's Journal, 142.

Hutchinson was also growing while the clergy were becoming more determined to enforce a strict Puritan orthodoxy in Puritan towns. The government during this period also dealt with Roger Williams for his anti-government views and caused him to flee for his life to Rhode Island in the midst of winter, February, 1634. Disputes with Plimoth over Connecticut and common borders in Massachusetts were also brewing. More importantly, in England, Thomas Morton and Sir Ferdinando Gorges had made good progress in their lawsuits against Massachusetts Bay, threatening the very charter to which the Puritans owed their government and existence in New England. Nevertheless, Puritans and other non-conformists continued to leave England, with thousands making New England their destination. In addition, the rivers in Connecticut were filled with Dutch, Swedish and independent English traders, while French were encroaching upon English posts in Maine. On the high seas, a sense of lawlessness prevailed, further complicating life for the Native Americans and colonists. Like Captain Hunt, many of the foreign fishing vessels were often pirates, their ships cruising the waterways looking for easy prey. As a result a strong criminal element had also taken up residence in the colony, a presence which tended to be overlooked by the Puritans because of the obvious need for men with these skill sets and rapacity. These were days of extreme difficulty for the new colony, and from the Puritan point of view, a time for heightened vigilance against their foes, presumed and otherwise. The ongoing trend in the new Puritan order was, therefore, to tighten up and take control, and not to buckle to any external nor internal pressures.

Despite Winthrop's effort to control the events in Connecticut, the situation rapidly deteriorated as the Puritans decided, even in the absence of a signed treaty, to increase their already impossible demands upon the Pequots. At the same time, the Pequots signaled to Winthrop their absolute refusal to return the persons responsible for the killing of Stone, claiming that they were not the perpetrators in the case; later evidence shows that the killings took place on the Connecticut River at a place occupied by Western Niantics, a tributary tribe of the Pequots. Winthrop was probably aware of the discrepancy in the charge, especially since his son, John Winthrop Jr., later erected his fort at the mouth of the Connecticut River, right in the middle of Western Niantic territory.

In the end, however, it was not political maneuvering which caused the eventual outcome – war with the Pequots. It was the killing of an English trader named John Oldham and several of his crew on a trading voyage to Block Island by Niantic Native Americans allied with the Narragansetts. After a period of repeated calls from the pulpit, Massachusetts Bay finally sent an expedition led by John Endicott to exact revenge. Failing to locate the perpetrators on Block Island, however, the Endicott expedition turned its fury on a Pequot village on the mainland, fully aware that they were not the responsible party. Forcing the residents to flee, Endecott ordered the village burned down and its crops stolen or destroyed. The Puritan's intentions were now clear to the Pequots, who undoubtedly saw themselves cut off and without any possible recourse other than war to counteract the injustice, kidnappings, violent attacks insults and incursions.

It is clear from all the evidence that the Puritans intended to subdue the Pequots and expropriate most of their land. A treaty would not suffice to obtain these goals. Even the Pequots obeisance to Puritan power apparently did little to defer the hostility of Puritan colonists, along with a theological critique which projected demonic qualities upon the Pequots. Every step taken by the Pequots was measured against this typologically derived standard. Even submission of the Pequots could not work within this theological paradigm, for the Puritans could not perceive themselves as the aggressors, rather the victims. But the facts belie the Puritan claim that the war was the result of demonic powers working amongst the Native Americans. It is obvious from testimonies and other evidence that Pequots were willing to allow English farms in their territory, showing that land was not really the only major objective of Puritan imposition in Connecticut. Actually, political control was the more important objective. Treaties implied that both sides were equal, and that could never be the case here. John Eliot had seen this earlier, and had been right in opposing Puritan aggression in Connecticut. For Puritans, a treaty was no more than a device to delay that which was already inevitable.

In 1635, a group of settlers from Dorchester became the first to break ranks and move to Connecticut. Soon after, Hooker and his congregation in New Towne (Cambridge) joined them. In their trail, a stream of Puritans and others followed, anxious to start planting their farms and establishing towns in the fertile river plains along the banks of the Connecticut River. It posed a dilemma for Massachusetts Bay. Hooker's followers, unwilling to submit themselves unswervingly to the control of Massachusetts Bay, were better situated to build a power base at Wethersfield than the Saybrook settlement at the mouth of the river and next to the Pequots.

In this context of conflicting interests, a period of heightening tensions, suspicions, and violent flare-ups resulted. Most English accounts blame the Pequots for initiating raids and threats against newly arriving settlers. But the new settlers had come prepared for battle, just as had their Massachusetts and Plimoth forbears. Taunts and scares would not deter them. The Pequot leaders, also determined not to let the English wrest control from them, continued to refuse to submit to the escalating demands made by Massachusetts Bay. Then, in June, 1636, suspicions would be amped up even more when supposed intelligence information came from the Mohegan sachem, Uncas, warning that the Pequots intended to attack the new settlements. Uncas, however, was a bitter rival and enemy of the coastal Pequots, with undoubtedly many reasons to double cross them. Aligning his people with the English appears to have been precisely that kind of gesture.

While the practical reasons for a war of conquest against the Pequots mounted in Puritan minds, a theological rationale for the coming battle was also forming in the Puritan religious imagination. In Massachusetts Bay, a strict theocracy required that all political thinking and laws must conform to the Mosaic ideal and patterns established in the Bible, and exceed them in their perfection. This perfectionist ideal also pertained to the matter of war, and we find the Puritans seldom in self-doubt because of their inner convictions. One of the foremost Puritan writers of the era, Edward Johnson, portrayed the brewing conflict through the typological lens of Puritan theology. Johnson's depiction is quite unique. Ignoring the practical considerations like the killing of Captain Stone, the delicate negotiations, and the escalated demands of the Massachusetts Bay government on the Pequots, he focuses instead on the "barbarous" character of the Pequot people. Beyond that, no rationale nor a consideration of just cause were needed. In literature from the period, it is this negative appraisal of the people themselves which offers itself up a reason to go to war. Johnson is not just maligning Pequots in the following diatribe, but is also creating a negative myth of the Pequots by projecting them into the middle of a fantastic metaphysical struggle:

> The great Jehovah, minding to manifest the multitude of his Mercies to the wandering Jacobites, and make an introduction to his following wonders, causeth the darke clouds of calamities to gather about them, presaging some terrible tempest to follow, With eyes full anguish, they face to the right, upon the damnable doctrines, as so many dreadful Engines set by Satan to intrap their poore soules; Then casting forth a left hand looke, the labour and wants accompaning a Desert, and terrible Wilderness affright them. Their memories minding them of their former plenty, it much aggravated the present misery, When with thoughts of recumbrances and deepe distresses of a dangerous Ocean hinders their thoughts of flight, besides the sterne looke of the Lordly Prelates, which would give them a welcome home in a famishing prison. ...These Native Americans trusting in their great Troopes, having feasted their corps in a ravening manner, and leaving their fragments for their Squawes, they sound an alarum with a full mouth, and lumbring voyce, and soone gather together without presse or pay, their quarrell being as antient as Adams time, propagated from that old enmity betweene the Seede of the Woman, and the Seed of the Serpent, who was the grand signor of this war in hand, ...[46]

Johnson's writing provides insight into the Puritan sense of reality; they understood correctly that they were surrounded by potential enemies, but rather than accepting that one obvious fact, their religious imagination was coaxed into believing that they existed at the center of a great power vortex composed of demonic forces they could not fully

---

[46] Johnson, Edward, <u>Johnson's Wonder Working Providence</u>, 147-148.

understand. Their response to this nightmarish vision was to search for a theological method to provide a mystical key to understand their circumstances. On the verge of war, they found that "key" by projecting their experiences back in time, and identifying themselves with the ancient Hebrews, thus imbuing their experience, actions and survival with an aura of innocence. Contrarily, every act of Pequot violence would justify the conviction in the Puritan mind the Pequots were evil. As Neal Salisbury writes, "Having located Satan in the Pequot camp, the English forces could proceed without restraint."[47]

As a result of the Uncas report, Massachusetts Bay convened a meeting at Saybrook between themselves and representatives from the Pequots and Western Niantics in July, 1636. Present at the meeting was Sassious, sachem of the Western Niantics. Although minutes of the conference were not taken, it is known that the Puritans once again demanded that Stone's killers be turned over to them along with the inflated tribute payments which the Pequots had already refused to pay, a sum basically amounting to a veiled threat. Refusing to budge on their position, Ray Jennings gives a description of what transpired as a result:

> The Pequots had gone as far as their conceptions of honor and obligation permitted. The next move in this affair was up to their tributary Sassious, sachem of the Western Niantics. Under the pressure of Massachusetts ultimatum, Sassious improvised a diplomatic maneuver worthy of a Talleyrand. he "gave" his whole country to John Winthrop jr., personally; which is to say that, regardless of what he intended that act to mean in terms of ownership of real estate, it definitely transferred the Western Niantic's allegiance from the Pequots.[48]

The Pequot response to the apparent abandonment by their tributary tribe was a brilliant diplomatic move. Instead of contesting the realignment, the Pequots decided to accept the the decision of the neighboring West Niantics. They likely assumed that this act in itself

---

[47] Salisbury, Manitou and Providence, 220.
[48] Jennings, The Invasion of America, 205.

The Pequot Massacres

cleared them of having to deal with the Puritan demands vis-a-vis the killers of Capt. Stone, and it must have surprised them when the Massachusetts Bay government continued pressing for the killers of Stone when everyone knew they were Western Niantics, not Pequots. It is clear, from a modern perspective, that the intention and plan of the Puritans to subdue and subject the Pequots under their authority is revealed in the tactic, providing the Puritans immediate control over Connecticut. Further complicating the matter, if they had relinquished their demands against the Pequots at this point, it would have been a virtual act of ceding their claim in Connecticut to Hooker's people at Wethersfield.

The Pequots, however, also understood the art of diplomacy, and were far from powerless in the matter. Deciding not to contest the Western Niantics, they quickly neutralized the Puritan diplomatic maneuver and took away their initiative in the matter. All sides had to retreat in order to save face, and the results of the conference were basically nil. But a few days after the failed conference, a new incident gave Massachusetts a new opportunity to achieve their goal when a group of Block Island Narragansetts killed Captain John Oldham, a member of the Massachusetts Bay colony. The motive for the murder was supposedly that the Narragansetts believed Oldham to have been responsible for spreading smallpox during an earlier trading mission by Oldham in their territory. Massachusetts Bay, however, used the incident as a ploy to draw themselves and the Pequots into a sharper dispute.

In response to the killing of Oldham, Massachusetts Bay sent out a military expedition under John Underhill to retaliate against the Narragansett aligned Block Island Native Americans. Underhill's expedition, however, failed when they arrived at the expected battleground only to find the majority of the tribe had fled into the swamps for refuge. The English soldiers were not used to fighting in swamps and woods, and their attempts to discover the Native Americans in their hiding places were unsuccessful. In frustration, Underhill's contingent then turned toward the coast of Connecticut to carry the battle to the Pequots instead, claiming that their stated purpose was to apprehend the murderers of Captain Stone. Most Puritan accounts of the episode are noteworthy in their failure to distinguish between the Block Islander Narragansetts and the Pequots. It is clear that Winthrop and the

Hidden Genocide, Hidden People

Massachusetts Bay government knew the difference for, upon hearing of the killing, they immediately lodged a protest with the leaders of the Narragansetts, the sachems Canonicus and Miantonomo. The Narragansetts, quick to apologize, demonstrated their good will toward the colony by sending an immediate expedition to Block Island to punish the perpetrators. This reveals the Puritan duplicity in the matter, being willing to overlook the murder of a respected citizen, Oldham, but unwilling to cede anything at all in the killing of Captain Stone. This tells us that, while the Puritans wanted control in Rhode Island, the real battleground was Connecticut, where the new settlers were chafing at the bit to go against the Pequots. The Oldham killing was a convenient excuse for the Puritans to beat their war drums, but not enough to declare war.

From Block Island, Underhill's forces sailed to the Saybrook fort where they remained for several days. From there, the expedition went out to confront the Pequots. Heavily armed and sailing along the coast in Pequot country, Underhill related an encounter with the Pequots:

> The Native Americans spying of us came running in multitudes along the water side, crying, What cheer, Englishmen, what cheer, what do you come for? They not thinking we intended war, went on cheerfully until they came to Pequot River. We thinking it the best way, did forbear to answer them; first that we might the better be able to run through the work; secondly, that by delaying of them, we might drive them in security, to the end we might have the more advantage of them. but they seeing we would make no answer, kept on their course, and cried, What, Englishmen, what cheer, what cheer, are you hoggery, will you cram us? That is, are you angry, will you kill us, and do you come to fight? That night the Western Niantic Indians, and the Pequots, made fire on both sides of the river, fearing we would land in the night. They made most doleful and woeful cries allnight, (so that we could scarce rest) hallooing one to another, and giving the word from place to place, to gather their forces together, fearing the English were come to

The Pequot Massacres

war against them.[49]

Underhill returned to Massachusetts Bay with the news of his failed campaign with both the Block Islanders and Pequots. Dissatisfied with the results, the government decided to press its demands with an ultimatum. First, they decided to play a hidden hand by turning to the Narragansetts for help against the stubborn Pequots. In the proceedings against the Pequots, the mark of John Winthrop is especially evident. This is especially true in the successful effort to win the support of the Narragansetts, which he did through his friend, Roger Williams. When Williams was banished, Winthrop had kept a regular contact with the exiled minister, and provided him some help with financial matters. Williams' close friendship with the Narragansetts was of great service to Winthrop as he attempted to build an alliance between the powerful tribe and Massachusetts Bay. Seizing the opportunity, Winthrop and the magistrates invited the Narragansett sachem, Miantonomo, to Boston, where they discussed the possibility of working together to defeat the Pequots. The Narragansetts, who had reasons of their own to oppose the Pequots, agreed to enter the proposed alliance by ratifying a treaty. Below are Winthrop's personal notes on the meeting combined with a copy of the treaty.

> After dinner, Miantunnomoh declared what he had to say to us in propositions, which were to this effect: That they had always loved the english and desired firm peace with us:
> - The Articles
> 1. A firm peace between us and our friends of other plantations, (if they consent,) and their confederates, (if they will observe the articles, etc.,) and our posterities.
> 2. Neither party to make peace with the Pequods without the other's consent.
> 3. Not to harbor, etc., the Pequods, etc.
> 4. To put to death or deliver over murderers, etc.

---

[49] John Underhill, "Newes From America", in History of the Pequot War, The Contemporary Accounts of Mason, Underhill, Vincent and Gardener, Charles Orr, ed. (Cleveland: The Helman-Taylor Company, 1897), 55.

5. To return our fugitive servants, etc.
6. We to give them notice when we go against the Pequods, and they to send us some guides.
7. Free trade between us. [50]

The treaty with the Narragansetts had the effect of defusing any tensions left over from the murder of John Oldham. However, the political situation between Puritans and Pequots was deteriorating, and the Narragansetts would soon be asked by Massachusetts Bay to provide more than guides, indeed warriors to fight the Pequots. Already, settlers in Connecticut were clamoring for battle, with John Mason and a corps of trained soldiers ready to move. The Pequots were well aware of the preparations. By late in the year, a number of minor skirmishes between English and Pequots took place wherein there were several injured or killed on both sides. Not surprisingly, in almost all the English accounts of prewar violence, the Pequots are shown to be the instigators, while the English actions are viewed innocently. Of course, any actions taken by the Pequots were regarded as signs of aggression rather than protective actions by the English and, it might be inferred vice versa. One incident for example, demonstrates how perfidious this logic was as it affected both sides in the conflict. Early in 1637, a group of Pequots surrounded the English fortifications at Saybrook, and held it under siege for several days. The affair was just one in a series of incidents, but it reveals a level of animosity and bad will which seems not to have existed earlier by Lt. Lion Gardener, who served as Commander of the Saybrook fort during the siege, reported the following dialogue:

> Then they said, Have you fought enough? We said we knew not yet. Then they asked if we did use to kill women and children? We said they should see that hereafter. So they were silent a small space, and then they said, We are Pequits, and have killed Englishmen, and can kill them as mosquetoes, and we will go to Conectecott and kill men, women and children, and we will take away the horses cows and hogs.[51]

---

[50] Winthrop, John Winthrop's Journal, vol. I, 193.
[51] Lion Gardener, "Relation of the Pequot Warres", in History of the Pequot War, 132.

The Pequot Massacres

The spring of 1637 found both Puritans and Pequots engaged in frantic preparations for the war which both knew was coming. Isolated outbreaks of violence continued to occur between the two parties. It was also during this time that the Pequots were reported to have sent a delegation to the Narragansetts to invite them into an alliance against the English, but the Narragansetts rejected the offer, probably through the influence of Roger Williams. The Narragansetts had been in a state of war with the Pequots since 1633, when approximately six thousand Narragansetts were killed in a horrible smallpox epidemic. The Pequots had capitalized on the Narragansetts' sudden weakness and had sent raiding parties into their territory. As a result, there was little trust between the two tribes, and a confederacy between the two rivals was not to happen. Instead, the Narragansetts remained faithful to the treaty which they had entered into with the English.

The Pequots, for their part, continued to resist the treaty conditions and further antagonize the English through verbal insults. Worse, the Pequots also insulted the god of the English. Johnson describes an encounter between Pequots and Puritans at Saybrook wherein the Pequots "blasphemed the Lord, saying Englishmans God was all one Flye, and that English man was all one Squyawe, and themselves all one Moor-hawws."[52] The fact that Johnson emphasized the above encounter demonstrates how deeply offensive such insults were to the Puritans.

Considering how ready and willing the Puritans were to persecute and/or banish non-conforming Christians such as Anne Hutchinson and Roger Williams, one can easily imagine the Puritan outrage at the insults rendered by the Pequots. After all, there were crimes and there were terrible crimes from the Puritan perspective, and among the very worst was the crime of blasphemy. In the first draft of New England's first set of laws, written by John Cotton, the first capital crime is listed and described as "blasphemy, which is a cursing of God by atheism, or the like, to be punished with death."[53]

In the spring of 1637, Roger Williams became involved with the Pequot issue on behalf of the Massachusetts Bay Colony. Although Williams has often been described as a "friend to the Native Americans", he appears to have been no friend to the Pequots, likely a result of his dependence and friendship with the Narragansetts. It is also likely that

Hidden Genocide, Hidden People

he shared this attitude with Rev. John Eliot, who had been admonished two years earlier for his criticism of the government policy toward the Pequots. Indeed, the Pequots were perceived to be a powerful nation by most English in the region and their territory included the best farmland in New England. Thus, it is not surprising that John Winthrop, Sr. would solicit aid from his friend, Roger Williams, despite Williams having been exiled from Massachusetts. Nevertheless, Williams became an important operative in the war by serving as a strategist, negotiator, interpreter and intelligence gatherer. Williams was also influential in persuading the Narragansetts to join in a combined force with Massachusetts Bay, Plimoth and Hartford to attack the Pequots.

Without Williams and his professed animosity toward the Pequots, it is doubtful that the war against the Pequots would have been so successful, for it was Williams' information and interventions which would ultimately give the English the advantage in the attack. The following are portions from a letter written by Williams to Henry Vane (Governor) and John Winthrop (Deputy Governor) in May 1637, and it demonstrates both Williams' and the Narragansetts' shared commitment to assure a military victory over the Pequots:

> Sir,
>
> The latter end of the last week I gave notice to our neighbour princes of your intentions and preparations against the common enemy, the Pequts. At my first coming to them, Caunounicus (morosus aeque ac barbarus senex) was very sour, and accused the English and myself for sending the plague amongst them, and threatening to kill him especially.
>
> Such tidings (it seems) were lately brought to his ears by some of his flatterers and our will-willers. I discerned cause of bestirring myself, and staid the longer, and at last (through the mercy of the Most High) I not only sweetened his spirit, but possest him, that the plague and other sicknesses were alone in the hand of the one God, who made him and us, who being

---

52 Johnson, Wonder-Working Providence, 164.
53 An Abstract of the Laws of New England, chap. 7

displeased with the English for lying, stealing, idleness and uncleanness, (the natives' epidemical sins,) smote many thousands of us ourselves with general and late mortalities.

Miantunnomu kept his barbourous court lately at my house, and with him I have far better dealing. He takes some pleasure to visit me, and sent me word of his coming over again some eight days hence.

They pass not a week without some skirmishes, though hitherto little loss on either side. They were glad of your preparations, and in much conference with themselves and others, (fishing de industria for instructions from them) I gathered these observations which you may please (as cause may be) to consider and take notice of:

1. They conceive that to do execution to purpose on the Pequts, will require not two or three days and away, but a riding by it and following of the work to and again the space of three weeks or a month, that there be a falling off and a retreat, as if you were departed, and a falling on again within three or four days, when they are returned again to their houses securely from their flight.

2. That if any pinnaces come in ken, they presently prepare for flight, women and old men and children, to a swamp some three or four miles on the back of them, a marvellous great and secure swam, which they called Ohomowauke, which signifies owl's nest, and by another name, Cuppacommock, which signifies a refuge or a hiding place, as I conceive.

3. That therefore Nayantaquit (which is Miantunnomue's place of rendezvous) be thought on for the riding and retiring to of vessel or vessels, which place is faithful to the Nanhiggonticks and at present enmity with the Pequts.

4. They also conceive it easy for the English, that the provisions and munition first arrive at Aquednetick,

called by us Rode-Island, at the Nanhiggontick's mouth, and then a messenger may be despatched hither, and so to the [Massachusetts] bay, for the soldiers to march up by land to the vessels, who otherwise might spend long time about the came and fill more vessels than needs.

5. That the assault would be in the night, when they are commonly more secure and at home, by which advantage the English, being armed [i.e., wearing armour], may enter the houses and do what execution they please.

6. That before the assault be given, an ambush be laid behind them, between them and the swamp, to prevent their flight, etc.

7. That to that purpose such guides as shall be best liked of be taken along to direct, especially two Pequts, viz. Wequash and Wuttackquiackommin, valiant men, especially the latter, who have lived these three or four years with the Nanhiggonticks, and know every pass and passage amongst them, who desire armour to enter their houses.

8. That it would be pleasing to all natives, that women and children be spared, etc.

9. That if there be any more land travel to Qunnihticutt, some course would also be taken with the Wunnashowatuckoogs, who are confederates with and a refuge to the Pequts.

Sir, if any thing be sent to the princes, I find that Canounicus would gladly accept of a box of eight or ten pounds of sugar, and indeed he told me he would thank Mr. Governour for a box full.[54]

The letter shows that Williams' objectives were practical, rising out of a concern for the vitality of the Narragansetts, assuming that a military foray into Connecticut would quell the rebellious Pequots and prevent further incursions against the weakened Narragan-

---

[54] Glenn W. LaFantasie, ed., The Correspondence of Roger Williams, vol. I (Hanover, NH: University Press of New England, 1988), 72-74.

setts. Given the cultural and political context, some might even perceive a moral tone in Williams' words, particularly in his request that "women and children be spared." One also wonders if Williams was privy to the overall strategy of Massachusetts Bay leaders, wherein instead of one army of "Jacobites", there would be seven, including Massachusetts Bay, Massachusetts, Plimoth, Connecticut, the Mohegans, Eastern Niantics and Narragansetts, all of whom were prevailed upon to send soldiers and warriors. Despite this amalgam of forces, it was the lightly armed Connecticut colony which finally preempted the others by first declaring war against the Pequots on May 1, 1637.

The Connecticut settlers upset the Massachusetts Bay plan to wait for the Pequots to make the first move, in order to label their own action as a defensive response. The Connecticut settlers made no such pretense, and lost no time in recruiting a small army of ninety volunteers under Captain John Mason, along with seventy five warriors from the local Mohegan tribe, led by the famous sachem, Uncas. With Connecticut firmly committed to "offensive war", Massachusetts Bay was forced to declare war as well, but now the situation had evolved beyond their control, requring their immediate action in order to regain preeminance in the region. Here, they had what could be called the proverbial 'ace up their sleeve' in Roger Williams. Using the information provided by Williams, the joint forces set forth to implement a plan which would lead to the massacre of a large portion of the Pequot nation.

The Puritan forces selected the Pequot town at Mystic as their first target because of its vulnerability, knowing that many Pequot warriors were away from the town at the time, with the majority of the population at home being women, children, and elders. As it was throughout this short and brutal war, the Puritan strategy emphasized surprise, unrestricted violence, but perhaps more importantly, a theological imperative. Throughout the campaign, the gathered soldiers certainly heard speeches from eminent clergy whom, as the law required, had accompanied them into the theater of battle. The following is the text of a sermon delivered as the soldiers prepared to pursue fleeing Pequot survivors. It is recorded below because it shows both the intensity of Puritan religious fervor and a certain 'blood lust' associated with it. The words were recorded by Puritan writer, Edward Johnson, although the author of the sermon remains unknown:

> Fellow-Souldiers, Country-men, and Companions in this Wildernesse worke, who are gathered together this day by the inevitable providence of the great Jehovah, not in a tumultuous manner hurried on by the floating fancy of every high hot headed braine, whose actions prove abortive, or if any fruit brought forth, it hath been rape, theft, and murther, things inconsisting with natures light, then much lesse with a Souldiers valour; but, by deare hearts, purposely pickt out by the godly grave Fathers of this government, that your prow esse may carry on the work, where there Justice in her righteous course is obstructed, you need not question your authority to execute those who God, the righteous Judge of all the world, hath condemned for blaspheming his sacred Majesty, and murthering his Servants; every comon Souldier among you is now installed a Magistrate; then shew your selves men of courage. I would not draw low the height of your enemies hatred against you, and so debase your valour. This you may expect, their swelling pride hath laid the foundation of large conceptions against you and all the people of Christ in this wildernesse, even as wide as Babels bottome. But, by brave Souldiers, it hath mounted already to the clouds, and therefore it is ripe for confusion; also their crueltie is famously knowne, yet all true-bred Souldiers reserve this as a common maxime, cruelty and cowardize are unseparable companions; and in briefe, there is notheing wanting on your enemies part, that may deprive you of a compleat victory, onely their nimbleness of foot, and the unaccessible swamps and nut tree woods, forth of which your small numbers may intice, and industry compell them. And now to you I put the question, you would not fight in such a cause with an agile spirit, and undaunted boldnesse? yet if you look for further encouragement, I have for you; riches and

honour are the next to a good cause eyed by every Souldier, to maintain your owne, and spoile your enemies of theirs; although gold and silver be wanting to either of you, yet have you that to maintaine which is farre more precious, the lives, libertyes, and new purchased freedomes, priviledges, and immunities of the indeared servants of our Lord christ Jesus, and of your second selves, even you affectionated bosome-mates, together with the chiefe pledges of your love, the comforting contents of harmlesse pratling and smiling babes; and in a word, all the riches of that goodnesse and mercy that attends the people of God in the injoyment of Christ, in his Ordinances, even in this life; and as for honour, David was not to be blame for enquiring after it, as a due and recompence of that true valour the Lord hath bestowed on him: and now the Lord hath prepared this honour for you, oh you couragious souldiers of his, to execute vengeance upon the heathen, and correction among the people, to binde their Kings in chaines, and Nobles in fetters of Iron, that they may execute upon them the judgements that are written! this honour shall be to all his Saints. But some of you may suppose deaths stroke may cut you short of this: let every faithfull Souldier of Christ Jesus know, that the cause why some of his indeared Servants are taken away by death in a just warre (as this assuredly is) it is not because they should fall short of the honours accompanying such noble designes, but rather because earths honours are too scant for them, and therefore the everlasting Crown must be set upon their heads forthwith. Then march on with a cheerfull Christian courage in the strength of the Lord and the power of his might, who will forthwith inclose your enemies in your hands, make their multitudes fall under your warlike weapons, and your feet shall be set on their proud necks.[55]

---

[55] Johnson, Wonder Working Providence, 165-166.

The initial attack upon the Pequot town at Mystic was so brutal and misdirected that many of the Narragansetts refused to comply with it. In the first place, they had originally been told that Mystic was a secondary target with little strategic importance. Realizing that the town at Groton could not be easily taken, the Puritan forces had marched instead to Mystic without consulting their allies. The rest could only be described as a nefarious act of genocide. Upon cover of darkness in early morning, the forces attacked the town under Captain Mason's direction. It is estimated that somewhere between three and seven hundred Pequots lived in the community. Most sources disagree with each other as to actual numbers. But what is clear is that it was a massacre and total military victory for the English. Furthermore, the massacre undermined Pequot morale and eventually scattered them in a woeful retreat, fleeing westward along the Connecticut, though most were overtaken by English forces and brutally executed.

In the end, while the Puritan's Native American allies had participated in the actions against the Pequot, many of them appealed in protest to the English when they saw the extent of the carnage. John Underhill wrote about the Native American reluctance to engage in such brutality. He relates, "Our Indians came to us, and much rejoiced at our victories, and greatly admired the manner of Englishmen's fight, but cried Mach it, mach it; that is, It is naught, it is naught, because it is too furious, and slays too many men."[56] These pleas seemed to have little effect. For them, the war was framed as a spiritual contest between their god and the devil. Indeed, the Puritans not only condoned their own brutality, they actually glorified it. The following description of the infamous battle at Mystic reveals the theological rationale:

> Most courageously these Pequots behaved themselves. But seeing the fort was too hot for us, we devised a way how we might save ourselves and prejudice them. Captain Mason entering into a wigwam, brought out a firebrand, after he had wounded many in the house. Then he set fire on the west side, where he entered; myself set fire on the south end with a train of powder. The fires of both meeting in the

---

[56] John Underhill, "Newes From America; or A New and Experimentall Discoverie of New England", in <u>History of the Pequot War</u>, 77-81.

center of the fort, blazed most terribly, and burnt all in the space of half an hour. Many courageous fellows were unwilling to come out, and fought most desperately through the palisadoes, so as they were scorched and burnt with the very flame, and were deprived of their arms - in regard to the fire burnt their very bowstrings - and so perished valiantly. Mercy did they deserve for their valor, could we have had opportunity to have bestowed it. Many were burnt in the fort, both men, women, and children. Others forced out, and came in troops to the Native Americans, twenty and thiry at a time, whch our soldiers received and entertained with the point of the sword. Down fell men, women, and children; those that scaped us, fell into the hands of the Indians that were in the rear of us. It is reported by themselves, that there were about four hundred souls in this fort, and not above five of them escaped out of our hands. Great and doleful was the bloody sight to the view of young soldiers that never had been in war, to see so many souls lie gasping on the ground, so thick, in some places, that you could hardly pass along. It may be demanded, Why should you be so furious? (as some have said). Should not Christians have more mercy and compassion? But I would refer you to David's war. When a people is grown to such a height of blood, and sin against God and man, and all confederates in the action, there he hath no respect to persons, but harrows them, and saws them, and puts them to the sword, and the most terriblest death that may be. Sometimes the Scripture declareth women and children must perish with their parents. Sometimes the case alters; but we will not dispute it now. We have sufficient light from the Word of God for our proceedings.[57]

Repeatedly, we read echoes of the above sentiments of Underhill in other writers of the era, especially participants. John Mason, who

---

[57] Ibid., 84.

personally gave the order to slay any Native American who escaped the flames, children not excluded, later wrote in exuberant theological terms of the massacre, declaring that through its excesses, the Puritan god "laughed his Enemies and the Enemies of his People to scorn making [the Pequot] as a fiery Oven . . . Thus did the Lord judge among the Heathen, filling [Mystic] with dead Bodies."[58]

The Puritans pursued their brutal course against Native Americans even though many Puritans were aware that it was excessive. English explorers and settlers had exhaustively compared and contrasted Algonquin and English modes of warfare, and most agreed on a profound difference between the two. Roger Williams, probably the most notable authority from the period described Native American wars as "far less bloody and devouring than the wars in Europe."[59] Williams perspective is fully verified in Native American testimonies and oral tradition, along with archeological evidence, both of which demonstrate that the Algonquin tribes of southern New England rarely fought wars of conquest. Instead, wars were generally campaigns of retaliation as the Native Americans followed a strict code of lex talionis. By custom and general practice, retaliation required no more and no less than what justice entailed. Typically, involvement in warfare and hostilities was seen as a voluntary activity, both at an individual and collective level.

In comparison, European societies had long developed laws and traditions that were highly repressive of individual freedoms. Military obligations, including conscription and war taxes were regular parts of common life in Europe. Algonquin tribes, in comparison, did not conscript their warriors, nor did powerful towns require weaker ones to commit to war efforts. Indeed, most wars were actually temporary hostilities or extended feuds between clan groups, and were not conducted on the sweeping scales and lengthy durations of European engagements. In contrast to the practice of genocidal wars, Algonquin customs appear to have encouraged conflict resolution through intermarriage, trading ventures, and social exchanges (e.g., games and har-

---

[58] Mason, John, A Brief History of the Pequot War: Especially of the Memorable taking of their Fort at Mistick in Connecticut in 1637 (Boston: S. Kneeland & T. Green, 1736), 30.

59 Williams, Roger, A Key Into the Language of America, 131.

The Pequot Massacres

vest celebrations). In many cases, some groups might extend borders or subject their neighbors to tribute offerings such as furs, food, and wampum, though we have little concrete evidence to make determinations as to how Native Americans organized and conducted themselves previous to European intrusions.

The Pequot War had introduced a new level of brutality to a people who probably never imagined it could exist. It is also apparent that few Puritan leaders doubted the rightousness of their actions against the Pequots, and certainly not their violent outcome. John Winthrop, himself, did not display any obvious self-doubt in a dispassionate description of the massacre to William Bradford. However, it should be noted that Winthrop's estimate of the fatalities were greatly reduced in comparison to any others. Was he lying or did he receive an erroneous report himself? Although it is impossible to know for sure, it would appear from the discrepancy of the various reports that a concern for public relations may have motivated Winthrop to understate the extent of the massacre. One fact on which he seems to agree with other historians is that many of their Native American allies had been injured due to the confusion of battle. This too must have been a cause for political concern, and only a 'friendly fire' explanation was likely to suffice as an explanation for the unevenness in mortality. Only one Puritan lost his life in the battle. Following is Winthop's explanation:

> Our English from Connecticut, with their Indians, and many of the Naragansetts, marched in the night to a fort of the Pequods at Mistick, and besetting the same about break of the day, after two hour's fight they took it, (by firing it,) and slew therein two chief sachems, and one hundred and fifty old men, women, and children, with the loss of two English, whereof but one was killed by the enemy. Divers of the Indian friends were hurt by the English, because they had not some mark to distinguish them from the Pequods, as some of them had.[60]

Greatly dispirited over the news of their losses and fearful for their own lives, Sassacus and the other sachems, after decidedly losing the

---

[60] Winthrop, Winthrop's Journal, 220.

battle, at least determined to lead their people in flight. That flight was unsuccessful for most of them. Some were caught near Guilford, Connecticut, where the English cut off the heads of two sachems. Today, that area is referred to as Sachem's Head. The majority of the survivors fled and took refuge in a swamp west of New Haven. The English surrounded the swamp and a furious fight ensued with great losses to the Pequots. The battle finally ended with an English gesture to extend mercy to any who would or could walk peaceably out of the swamp. These few survivors, along with scant others who were lucky enough to escape the slaughter, were returned to their homeland to live out their lives in poverty and hardship, a burden that would be shifted repeatedly to their descendants for more than four centuries to come.

Chapter Four
The Spoils of War

> Awake! awake Ahasuerus, if there be any of thy seed or spirit here, and let not Haman destroy us as he hath done our Mordecai! And although there hath been much blood shed here in these parts among us, God and we know it came not by us. But if all must drink of this cup that is threatened, then shortly the king of Sheshack shall drink last, and tremble and fall when our pain will be past.[61]

The Puritans asserted their claims in New England based on the typological interpretations of a wide ranging assortment of Biblical references. However, the Pequot War, with all of its horrors and injustices, required an extra stretch of the religious imagination. For example, in Lion Gardener's words quoted above, we see this typology in practice by using the biblical figure of Haman to portray the defeated Pequots, and Mordecai to portray the Puritans. The casting of these two figures form the framework of the story of Esther, and is the central story in the Jewish holiday of Purim. In the story, Haman is an evil vizier to the Persian king, Ahasuerus, and plots to kill all the Jews. Here, the Pequots are portrayed as Haman. A Jewish man named Mordecai, with the aid of his adopted daughter, Queen Esther, manages to foil the plot and save their people. Of course, the Puritans in this typological construct are identified with the heroic figure of Mordecai. This demonizing of the Pequots and elevation of the spiritual status of the Puritans created a negative myth and provided a ready rationale for war and violent overthrow. Thus, Gardiner's words were meant to draw suspicion and incite hatred of the enemy, and to project upon them the most nefarious intention possible – an intention to kill all the Puritans.

So, the Puritans readily convinced themselves of the righteousness of the war against the Pequots. From their perspective, the results

---

61 Lion Gardiner, "Relation of the Pequot Warres", in <u>History of the Pequot War,</u> 147.

proved beyond doubt that their god was on their side. Furthermore, the victory over the Pequots occurred concurrently with the antinomian controversies in Boston; at the same time English soldiers and Native American allies were finishing their campaign against the Pequots, Puritan magistrates were engaged in persecuting Anne Hutchinson and her followers. So, in a sense, there were two wars taking place concurrently in New England, one against Native Americans and the other against dissenters. In this second war, when Hutchinson (seen as a ringleader of the dissenters) was finally convicted and banished, many Puritan clergy saw this as a divinely wrought victory as well. But this type of victory is seldom simple, bringing with it great costs and added complexity, although the Puritans obviously viewed it more simply – they thought they were now in full control. Defiance is a word which fits much Puritan writing about the war. Thomas Shepherd described the inner workings of a Puritan synod (meeting) and their attempt to impose a positive meaning by interpreting the twin events as an omen. Summarizing the synod's resolutions, he writes, "Thus the Lord having delivered the country from war with Native Americans and Familists, (who arose and fell together,) he was pleased to direct the hearts of magistrates, (then keeping Court ordinarily in our town, because of these stirs at Boston,) to think of erecting a School or College (Harvard), and that speedily, to be a nursery of knowledge in these deserts, and supply for posterity."[62]

Even as the Puritan synod was establishing Harvard, there was killing taking place. While virtually every Pequot had been displaced from their home, there was one group of Pequots left, including an estimated two hundred women and children and eighty men who had taken refuge in a swamp near Quinnipiac (New Haven), though the actual location has long been in dispute. This main body of Pequot refugees were led by the Pequot head sachem, Sassacus. In a flight westward, away from pursuing Puritans, the group had taken refuge in a swamp. The refuge turned out to be a death trap for most of them. The Pequots stood little chance as the English surrounded the swamp and were able to quickly destroy the stubborn group. Despite the carnage, Puritan leaders displayed little remorse over what took place there. Be-

---

[62] Thomas Shepard, "Memoir", in <u>Chronicles of the First Planters of the Colony of Massachusetts Bay From 1623-1636</u>, 550.

The Spoils of War

low is a portion of John Winthrop's graphic report to Governor William Bradford describing the massacre and mop-up operations (which included indiscriminate executions and slaveries of innocent people and children):

> Then our men cut off a place of swamp with their swords, & cooped up the Native Americans into a narrow compass, so as they could easier kill them through the thickets. So they continued all the night, standing about twelve foot one from another, & the Native Americans coming up close to our men, shot their arrows so thick, as they pierced their hat brims, & their sleeves & stockings, & other parts of their clothes; yet so miraculously did the Lord preserve them, as not one of them was wounded, save those there who rashly went into the swamp as aforesaid. When it was near day it grew very dark, so as those of them that were left, dropped away, though they stood but twelve or fourteen foot asunder, & were presently discovered, & some killed in the pursuit. In the searching of the swamp the next morning, they found nine slain, & some they pulled up, whom the Native Americans had buried in the mire; so as they do think that of all their company not twenty did escape, for they afterwards found some who died in the fight, of their wounds received. The prisoners were divided, some to those of the river, & the rest to us of these parts. We send the male children to Bermuda by Mr. William Pierce, & the women & maid children are disposed about in the towns. There have been slain & taken in all, about seven hundred, the rest are dispersed, & the Native Americans, in all quarters, so terrified, as all their friends are afraid to receive them. Two of the Sachems of Long Island came to Mr. Stoughton, & tendered themselves to be under our protection; & two of the Neposet Sachems have been with me to seek our friendship. Among the prisoners we have the wife & children of Mononotto, a woman

of very modest countenance & behaviour. It was by her mediation, that two English maids were spared from death, & ere kindly used by her. One of her first requests was, that the English would not abuse her body, & that her children might not be taken from her. Those which were wounded we fetched soon off, by John Gallop, who came with his boat in a happy hour, to bring them victuals, & to carry their wounded men to the barque, where our chief surgeon was, with Mr. Wilson, being about eight leagues off. Our people are all in health, the Lord be praised. And although they had marched in their arms all the day, & had been in fight all the night, yet they professed they found themselves so, as they would willingly have gone to such another business. The Captains report we have slain thirteen Sachems, but Sasacus & Mononotto are still living. This is the substance of what I have received, though I am forced to omit many considerable circumstances. So being in much straightness of time, the ships being to depart within this four days, & in them Lord Lee & Mr. Vane; I here break off & with hearty salutations, &c. I rest. [63]

Like John Winthrop, most Puritans saw the war's outcome as a fulfillment of Puritan destiny to achieve dominion over New England. "For many settlers, the Pequot slaughter was the ideological as well as military turning point in the war and in their conquest of New England.", states Neal Salisbury.[64] Most importantly, the combination of Puritan military might and ideology had forever altered the way of the Native American in New England. It brought rapid political, cultural, and economic change together with massive commercial exploitation. A precedent had been set which no Native American could afford to ignore in New England.

At the war's end, the most complicated issue facing Puritan leaders involved survivors, many of them women and children. Both the Nar-

---

[63] John Winthrop, "Letter to William Bradford, dated July 28, 1637", in Life and Letters of John Winthrop, vol. 2, 199-200.
[64] Salisbury, Manitou and Providence, 122.

ragansetts and the Mohegans petitioned the Puritans at Hartford and Massachusetts Bay for the right to adopt the Pequot survivors into their tribes, but the Puritans had already devised a plan to sell them into slavery or give them as gifts or gratuities to those who had participated in the war. While the English eventually agreed to a compromise, one of the tragic ironies of this episode is that there were not enough survivors to go around to satisfy everyone. Only a small remnant were allowed to stay in place as Pequots in their original territory, and the irony in this is that the remnants of the first exterminated Native American nation in New England actually survived into the modern age, while most others have disappeared.

As the Puritan forces consolidated their military hold upon the Pequot and Western Niantic lands, many tribes in the region saw no other option than to subject themselves to the Puritans. The Narragansetts were one notable exception, refusing to subject themselves to the primacy of Puritan rule. Instead, they took another tact, aware of the futility involved in trying to stem the tide of new English nonconformist refugees fleeing into their territory. For the Narragansetts, as well as others, the expedient choice was to sell their land, which had became the new trade commodity in southern New England, replacing the trade in furs as the mainstay of Native American economies. It would be impossible to determine from historical data whether Native Americans in New England were paid fairly, but the results speak for themselves. Native Americans who acquiesced to the Puritans paid a horrific price for that in the end.

With the addition of Connecticut to the Puritan political landscape, one of the immediate outcomes of the war was a reconfiguration of Puritan leadership. The major change was in Connecticut, where Thomas Hooker and his contingent succeeded quickly in establishing themselves as a force to be reckoned with in New England. Along with the Puritan settlers around Hartford, Uncas and his Mohegan tribe had also fought their way to power and influence by their alliance with Puritan forces. Uncas, often criticized by historians as devious and villainous, never deserted his Puritan allies. This alliance altered the shape of New England politics for another generation as well, with Uncas' warriors often fighting as agents of the English in military campaigns.

The war also opened up of the rest of the Connecticut shoreline for

Puritan acquisitions. The New Haven Colony was established in 1638 by a prosperous group of Puritans known as the Davenport Company, led by a minister named John Davenport and a wealthy merchant named Theophilus Eaton. The group came largely from the prominent St. Stephen's parish in London, and had intended to settle within the Massachusetts Bay patent. Failing to find a suitable harbor in which to establish themselves, they had turned their attention to Connecticut and the area inhabited by the Quinnipiacs, now known as New Haven. Although the Davenport Company lacked a patent, the establishment of a plantation at New Haven was accomplished with the support of Massachusetts Bay, partly because of Davenport's close friendship and association with John Cotton of Boston. Within a few years, the plantation prospered and expanded east to Stamford and west to Guilford, even staking a claim on the Delaware River. In 1643, the plantation officially became an independent colony. Its relationship to Massachusetts Bay remained close, and New Haven's first set of laws was adopted from those drafted by John Cotton for Massachusetts Bay.[65]

The Puritan victory also cleared the way for the next generation of settlers to penetrate the interior regions of Massachusetts along the Connecticut River. By the end of the seventeenth century, English agricultural settlements would extend as far north as the fertile lands of the Pocumtucks around Deerfield, Massachusetts. This expansion would have a calamitous impact upon the Native American population, unleashing new epidemics and undermining their culture and traditional subsistence economies.

As the upper Connecticut River towns continued to grow during the 1640's, so did the wealth, power, and influence of the first traders, particularly Pynchon, who owned tremendous plots of land which he rented out to land-hungry settlers. In addition, Pynchon acted as a financial backer to many enterprises and held a proprietary interest in the success of the new towns. His influence also helped the river towns to develop a certain amount of independence from their overseers in Boston. The value of land in New England was on a continual rise in value due to rapid immigration, and shrewd traders like Pynchon made a substantial profit in land purchases and sales. In addition, many un-

---

[65] Isabel M. Calder, "John Cotton and the New Haven Colony", The New England Quarterly, 3, no. 1, (1930): 87.

The Spoils of War

scrupulous traders lured Native Americans throughout New England into credit schemes in order to obtain desired goods. Most of the settlements were established through purchase agreements with local sachems. In many of these deals, the Native Americans retained hunting and fishing rights, a practice that must have seemed attractive at first to local sachems who viewed the economic arrangement as mutually advantageous. This attitude enabled a relatively benign coexistence between English and Native American towns, a relationship which would continue until the King Philip War.

The various Algonquin tribes of the upper Connecticut River had enjoyed a long period of continuous development for thousands of years. The rich alluvial soils along the river had allowed for abundant corn, squash, tobacco, beans and other crops. Upland meadows provided superb hunting with an abundance of turkey and other fowl. The river itself brought forth an abundance of fish to harvest, especially during the seasonal salmon runs. In places like Pawcumtuck, Northfield, Springfield, and others, the English were duly impressed by the fertility and pliability of the soils. New England, because of its rocky soil and hilly terrain, was not generally suitable for large scale agriculture, but the Connecticut River Valley was a notable exception.

From the English perspective, one of the disadvantages of settling the frontier regions in the upper reaches of the Connecticut River was the remoteness and vulnerability of the region. Nearby, there were also dozens of Native American towns. Nevertheless, these agricultural communities quickly developed, soon spreading up the Connecticut River as far north as Vermont. Despite the rapid development, the new settlements were separated from other Massachusetts Bay towns by over one hundred miles of rugged highland country occupied by the Nipmucs. A peaceful coexistence, therefore, was necessary for survival due to the relative weakness of the English communities.

The Pequot War also allowed for expansion along the eastern Connecticut shoreline, and allowed the Puritans, under Gov. John Winthrop, Jr., to expand into New London and further up the coast. However, beyond the former territory of the Pequots was the territory of the Eastern Niantics, a tributary tribe of the Narragansetts. Roger Williams' opposition to the encroachment demonstrated to the Narragansetts the value of an independent English presence in their territory as a hedge against Puritan domination. Therefore, the Narragansetts and their tributary tribes welcomed to their territories a steady stream of dissenters: Separatists, Baptists, Quakers, Antinomians and other non-conformists fleeing from persecution and intolerance in Massachusetts Bay. Through this arrangement, many English settlers and Narragansetts forged a strong bond based on both groups need to protect against the intrusive policies of their Puritan neighbors. Although the Massachusetts Bay Colony strongly opposed the establishment of a non-Puritan government in New England, its hands were tied because of the English government support of the non-conformists in Rhode Island.

The competition for the spoils of war would eventually become acrimonious. Since the Narragansetts were officially allies with Massachusetts Bay, any hostilities between the Narragansetts and Mohegans created difficulties between Massachusetts Bay and Hartford. Massachusetts Bay generally supported the Narragansetts in their disputes with Uncas and the Mohegans, not wanting them to assume too much power, resulting in an untenable position for them. They did not trust the Narragansetts either, although the Narragansetts had been faithful to their agreements over time and secure in their legal rights as English subjects. The real problem was that their support for the Narragansetts diminished the prospect of Massachusetts Bay to dominate their territory. It was a real dilemma. That is why, when a letter accusing the Eastern Niantics of conspiring to initiate attacks against English settlements arrived from Connecticut on September 1, 1641, the Massachusetts Bay authorities took ample precautions despite the dubious nature of the evidence. Below is John Winthrop's summary of the charges:

> There came letters from the court at Connecticut, and from two of the magistrates there, and from Mr. Ludlow, near the Dutch, certifying us that the Native Americans all over the country had combined themselves to cut off all the English, that the time was appointed after harvest, the manner also, they should go by small companies to the chief men's houses by way of trading, etc., and should kill them in the houses and seize their weapons, and then others should be at hand to prosecute the massacre: doesn't this prove the

> perfidiousness of their plot and that this was discovered by three several Native Americans, near about the same time and in the same manner; one to Mr. Eaton of New Haven, another to Mr. Ludlow, and the third to Mr. Haynes. This last being hurt near to death by a cart, etc., sent after Mr. Haynes, and told him that Englishman's God was angry with him, and had set Englisman's cow to kill him, because he had concealed such a conspiracy against the English, and so told him of it, as the other two had done. Upon this their advice to us was, that it was better to enter into war presently, and begin with them, and if we would send 100 men to the river's mouth of Connecticut, they would meet us with a proportionable number.[66]

Despite the Connecticut settlers' willingness to start another war, Winthrop and the Massachusetts Bay magistrates were hesitant to do more than take precautions. Upon receiving the report the General Court acted by disarming the two major Native American tribes in their region, a Massachusett village centered in Braintree led by Cutshamekin and the Penacooks led by Pasconoway. They also sent two agents directly to Miantonomo in order to question him regarding Narragansett intentions. Winthrop's reflections on the matter reveal the skepticism with which the Connecticut report was received by the Massachusetts Bay leaders:

> We spent the better part of two days in treating with him, and in conclusion he did accomodate himself to us to our satisfaction; only some difficulty we had, to bring him to desert the Nianticks, if we had just cause of war with them. They were, he said, as his own flesh, being allied by continual intermarriages, etc. But at last he condescended, that if they should do us wrong, as he could not draw them to give us satisfaction for, nor himself could satisfy, as if it were for blood, etc., then he would leave them to us.
>
> "When we should go to dinner, there was a table

---

66 Winthrop, <u>Winthrop's Journal</u>, vol. 2, 74.

> provided for the Native Americans, to dine by themselves, and Miantunnomoh was left to sit with them. This he was discontented at, and would eat nothing, till the governor sent him meat from his table. So at night, and all the time he staid, he sat at the lower end of the magistrate's table.[67]

While Governor Winthrop himself seemed to be satisfied with Miantonomo's answers, Connecticut continued to press the case against the Narragansetts despite a lack of evidence. There is no question in these proceedings that animosity between the Narragansetts and Mohegans was responsible for the rumors. Indeed, the Mohegans and Narragansetts continued to press their cases against each other for the next few decades through both raids and diplomatic initiatives. Massachusetts had every reason to discourage the war brewing between the two tribes, as they did not want to give reason for Connecticut to march into Rhode Island and claim it as a "prize" of war. That prerogative was definitely one which Massachusetts Bay wanted to reserve to itself. The situation probably would have lain dormant except that Connecticut appeared determined to precipitate another war. Winthrop reports the Massachusetts Bay reaction:

> And accordingly, letters were sent back to our brethren at Connecticut, to acquaint them with our opinions, and to dissuade them from going forth, alleging how dishonorable it would be to us all, that, while we were upon treaty with the Native Americans, they should make war upon them, for they would account their act as our own, seeing we had formerly professed to the Native Americans that we all as one, and in our late message to Miantunnomoh, had remembered him again of the same, and he had answered that he did so account of us. Upon receipt of the this our answer, they forbare to enter into war, but (it seemed) unwillingly, and as not well pleased with us.[68]

The tense standoff between Massachusetts Bay and Connecticut

---

[67] Ibid., 78.

continued to hold until Uncas' Mohegans made a move by attacking one of the Miantonomo's kinsmen in Connecticut, precipitating a major confrontation between the two tribes. Miantonomo appealed to Massachusetts Bay for permission to retaliate and was given approval. But later, in the course of a tense negotiation between Uncas and Miantonomo, violence broke out and Miantonomo was captured by the Mohegans wearing a suit of metal armor lent to him by one of Samuel Gorton's men. Uncas then took the Sachem to Hartford where the English kept him prisoner.

Uncas had presented the English with a captive, but also with a dilemma. Uncas was afraid of killing Miantonomo himself because Miantonomo was a 'political hot potato'. As a result, Miantonomo's fate was decided in a first meeting of the Commissioners of the United Colonies, the so-called infamous "Star Chamber" of the Puritans; here he was tried on the trumped-up charge of a treaty violation for not consulting with all the various Puritan governments, and for not going through the proper channels before taking his course of action. This decision was disingenuous since Miantonomo had indeed gone through the correct channels and had received the approval of Massachusetts Bay to retaliate against Uncas. Miantonomo was the victim of duplicity, and it was obvious to all involved, yet the Connecticut government held him prisoner, and proceeded to make what only could be considered a politically expedient decision.

The Commissioners' "resolution" was an especially nefarious form of state execution. While the Commissioners passed the death sentence, they ordered Uncas, the one who was conduct the execution outside of English territory; still, the execution was carried out under the observation of two English agents. The execution had a dual effect. First, it cemented the relationship of Uncas and the Hartford government. Second, it caused the Narragansett tribes to swear revenge against the treachery of Uncas in carrying out the gruesome business, and ruptured whatever trust the Narragansetts might have had in Massachusetts Bay. Thus Massachusetts rid itself of a faithful friend and ally. The whole episode probably deserves the epitaph pronounced upon it by George Bodge as "the most infamous decree which blots the pages of

---

[68] Ibid., 79.

new England history, condemned the brave Sachem of the noblest of the native tribes to a cruel and shameful death." [69]

To understand some of the Puritan animus for Miantonomo and the Narragansetts, one must also understand the relationship between Roger Williams and the Narragansetts. Williams had long debated with Massachusetts Bay leaders over Native American policies. When Williams himself entered into an agreement to purchase property around Providence, he did so in accordance with Narragansett customs rather than English, although a written deed of conveyance was also promulgated. Nevertheless, one of the concessions regarding the legal status of the deeds which Williams is said to have publicly reaffirmed, is that they were not intended to be permanent transfers of land, nor did they convey sovereignty. While English settlers were still subjects of the English King, Williams insisted that concessions needed to be made in deference to native culture and legal traditions. In this way and others, Williams respected and served the autonomy and interests of his Narragansett neighbors.

Williams had been both censured and exiled from Massachusetts, but banishment had little effect upon his outspokenness against the Puritan political order. During the next two decades, Williams argued through essays, pamphlets and letters for the renunciation of the theocratic Puritan government in Massachusetts. And while Williams' major criticisms focused on Puritan treatment of English Separatists, Baptists, Quakers, atheists and other non-conformists, much of his writing had a direct bearing on Native American relations. Williams went much further than merely criticizing the Massachusetts Bay colony. Williams was fundamentally critical of their reliance upon the royal patent, claiming that it conferred no rights beyond the established territories of England. Here, Williams' argument was made essentially on theological grounds rather than a political one. Glenn LaFantasie provides some helpful clarification, stating, "Williams' ideas about the patent may well have been influenced by his already close and sympathetic associations with the Native Americans of southern New England, but at the heart of his argument was a more fundamental, and theological point; the monarchs of England, he said, had no right to grant patents

---

[69] George Madison Bodge, Soldiars in King Philip's War, (Leominster, MA: Printed for the Author ,1896) 20.

of land in the name of Christendom because there was no such thing as Christendom."[70]

To understand Williams' ideas about religion and the state, it is helpful to compare his use of typology to that of Massachusetts Bay Puritanism. Williams, though he utilized typological method in Biblical interpretation himself, was harshly critical of Puritan theologians, especially John Cotton, with whom Williams would continue to exchange harsh and acrimonious words. Williams' disagreement with Cotton was over modes of biblical interpretation; he was especially critical of the assumption of the divine right of governance. Williams could see no justification either for the Puritans, nor the royalist claims of divine rights as well, following closely in the steps of his mentor in England, Sir Edward Coke. It was Coke who popularized the saying, "a man's house is his castle". Coke was the preeminent spokesperson of his time in arguing for the sovereign right of the individual. We can see Coke's theories reflected in William's ideas of 'soul liberty' and 'freedom of conscience', which he developed in his years in Rhode Island. But Williams went even further than Coke, speaking to the matter of liberty in purely theological terms. Sacvan Bercovitch analyzed the two different approaches represented by Cotton and Williams and concluded that, "the conflict stood between two views of typology, which might be called the allegorical and the historical modes." [71] In effect, Williams' allegorical approach placed the emphasis upon inner spiritual development, while the historical approach assumed foreknowledge of god's plan based upon an interpretation of past events.

For Williams, the state should never be identified with nor compromised by any religion. He believed that it was wrong to impose religious standards of belief and behavior that had nothing to do with the need for public order and protection of individuals. John Cotton, on the other hand, along with many other leading Puritans of his day, utilized a historical approach based in eschatological reasoning, seeing the Puritan enterprise as a key development toward the establishment of a divine order in human society. Berkovitch again is helpful in draw-

---

[70] Glenn W. LaFantasie, ed., The Correspondence of Roger Williams, (Hanover, NH: Univesity Press of New England,1988), 15.

[71] Sacvan Bercovitch, "Typology in Puritan New England", William and Mary Quarterly , 19, (1967): 175.

Hidden Genocide, Hidden People

ing out the implications of Cotton's methodology:

> Cotton proclaims the literal-spiritual continuity between the two Testaments and the colonial venture in America. In effect, he posits an historic movement in which New England, Israel's antitype (by way of Christ), becomes in turn a preview of the New Jerusalem. Though he never says so as explicitly as does Williams, he is delineating a form of typology which links past, present and future in a developmental historiography.[72]

Cotton's typology was based on comparisons between the Puritan Commonwealth and the biblical prototypes from ancient Israel and Judaea. But how did this typological method deal with such an extraordinary event such as the Pequot War? For the Puritans, the defeat of the Pequots was a fulfillment of eschatological proportions. It was not merely a battle between two societies with conflicting interests, although from a public relations perspective, the Puritans made a strong case for it being a war of retribution. The Puritans needed a spiritual explanation for genocide. Therefore, the Puritan rationale suggested that the actions taken against the Pequots were actually much more cosmic and grand than an ordinary war, and stood as an omen of ultimate victory of good over evil. Perhaps that is why John Mason, who gave the order to burn the Pequots in their houses, could exult with so much certainty over the fate of his fallen enemy:

> Thus was God seen in the Mount, Crushing his proud Enemies and the Enemies of his People: They who were ere while a Terror to all that were round about them, who resolved to Destroy all the English and to Root their very Name out of this Country, should by such weak Means, even Seventy seven (there being no more at the Fort) bring the Mischief they plotted, and the Violence they offered and excercised, upon their own Heads in a Moment: burning them up in the fire of his Wrath, and dunging the Ground with their Flesh: It was the Lord's Doings and it is marvel-

---

[72] Ibid., 176.

lous in our Eyes. It is He that hath made his Work wonderful, and therefore ought to be remembered.[73]

It is clear that theological animus is driving Mason's rhetoric in this passage, along with a lack of compassion, moral awareness or reasoning. One should not be surprised, considering the context. Those who have committed such heinous acts in other situations have typically shown similar characteristics and ability to justify genocide. "Remorse is for children.", stated Adolph Eichmann about his attitude to the atrocities and exterminations he ordered against Jews and other minorities in Nazi Europe. The difference in Mason's writing is the tendency to write in exalted terms about the genocide of the Pequots, a thoroughly and despicably inhumane act, particularly in the intentional murder of children and other innocents. Here, the Puritan god is invoked in the diatribe, not just supporting the violence, but actively engaged in the slaughter of innocents. Even Eichmann didn't claim as much. The real issue lies in the conception of theocratic government embraced by the Puritans, and the outrageous and extreme distortion of human values engendered by its loosely conferred authority. While Mason's rhetoric does not imply a particular typological comparison, it is clearly based in typological method. This tendency can be found throughout the Puritan literature of its time. The fusion of apocalyptic vision and temporal reality presented in Mason's account of the massacre is consistent with Puritan typological method, a highly transformative and pliable means of doing theology in that period.

Typological method is also dominant in the conception of civil codes in early Massachusetts Bay, particularly in their draconian adherence to punishments, including torture and executions. When John Cotton wrote the first version of <u>An Abstract of the Lawes of New-England</u>, also referred to as the *Cotton Code*, he based his formulations on Biblical precepts dependent upon a typological ordering of scripture passages. According to the *Cotton Code*, a fundamental role of government was "to preserve religion."[74] But the "Cotton Code" went even further than this basic definition, setting harsh punishments for opposing its authority and claims. While the code was claimed to have been based solely on scripture, its genesis was the perceived need

---

[73] John Mason, "A Brief History of the Pequot War", in <u>History of the Pequot War</u>, 35.

Hidden Genocide, Hidden People

for discipline in the new Puritan society. The Puritans generally believed themselves to be surrounded by evil; they worked incessantly at ways to destroy it, and they were very inventive in the means which they used. For taking the name of God in vain, Cotton wrote, "With corporall punishment either by stripes, or by branding him with a hot iron, or boring through the tongue, who hath bored and pierced God's name."[75] In recasting the ancient criminal codes of the Old Testament world, the Puritans set up a formidable hedge against the rest of the world, a hedge constructed of violence, threats and forebodings. But the hedge was not just physical; it was also mystical. Only the select few were chosen and rewarded, and those on the outside were acceptable only so far as they might promote or be drawn into the Puritan cause. If they posed a burden or danger to that cause, they were punishable or expendable.

The "Cotton Code" also provided a means for prosecuting wars. Cotton proposed, "First, A Law is to be made (if it be not made already) for the trayning of all men in the Countrey fit to beare armes unto the exercise of military Discipline; and withall another Lawe to be made for the maintenance of military Officers and Forts."[76] He proposed further, "The spoyles got by warre are to be divided into two pars, between the Souldiers and the Commonwealth that sent them forth.", he continues.[77] The "Cotton Code" was based upon a selective typology, but it clearly reflected the specific pragmatic concerns of the Puritan commonwealth.

Williams never stopped arguing against Cotton's precept that the state could somehow be suffused with God's will through the church, and therefore responsible for the maintenance of both civil and religious affairs. To Williams, such an idea was antithetical to the true nature of the church, which was spiritual rather than temporal. Therefore, Williams continued to battle Cotton over what he believed was the presumptuousness of his typological interpretations, vociferously opposing the notion of a national church or national covenant. To Wil-

---

[74] John Cotton, "An Abstract of the Lawes of New England", in John Cotton, The New England Way , 3.
[75] Ibid.14.
[76] Ibid. 6.
[77] Ibid. 17.

The Spoils of War

liams, this was a fraudulent concept which encouraged an arrogant abuse of power in the persecution of non-conformers. Thus, he reiterated over and over again in his published responses to Cotton that the civil authorities had no right nor mandate to act in God's name nor to presume to carry out God's will through persecutions and the shedding of blood. "It is righteous", Williams wrote, "for the Magistrates to defend their subjects in their civil Rights, for it is within the compass of his calling, being essentially civil: And unless we also grant him a spiritual calling and office (which is the Point denied) tis beyond his calling and compass to judge of what is Spiritual Right and wrong, and accordingly to pass a Spiritual sentence, and execute and inflict spiritual punishment."[78]

In a manner, Williams practiced what he preached. Although Williams found the religious practices of his neighboring Narragansetts greatly to his distaste, he refused to render judgment nor actively proselytise himself. This in itself, was reminiscent of his Narragansett neighbor's convictions, which Williams obviously respected. "They have a modest Religious perswasion not to disturb any man, either themselves, English, Dutch, or any in their Conscience, and worship.", he wrote.[79] Williams was obviously satisfied to return the gesture, and maintained this position throughout his later career. Unlike the Puritans, Williams and many other settlers in Rhode Island had reached an accommodation with the Narragansetts based on practical considerations and a respect for their rights and customs. It is especially noteworthy and ironic that these customs also coincided with Williams' theological beliefs. This was a direct affront in itself to the policies of Puritan Massachusetts which depended upon Biblical and legal mandates to interpret its relationship to the Native Americans.

The publishing of Williams' Narragansett/English dictionary and cultural study, A Key into the Language of America, provides a key to understanding the success of the Rhode Island experiment. Williams discovered traits in the Narragansetts which most other English

---

[78] Roger Williams. The Bloudy Tenent, Of Persecution. in The Complete Writings of Roger Williams, vol. III., Samuel L. Caldwell, ed., (Publications of the Narragansett Club: Providence, R.I. 1867), 276.

[79] Roger Williams. A Key into the Language of America. (Providence, RI: The Roger Williams Press,1936), 129.

Hidden Genocide, Hidden People

colonists did not affirm or approve. One of these traits, generosity, had been obvious from the start when Massasoit came with his people laden with gifts of corn and other provisions for Plimoth. There was a basic greed and stinginess which pervaded Christian Europe in comparison, and Williams was bold to point this out. "It is a strange truth," he observes, "that a man shall generally find more free entertainment and refreshing amongst these Barbarians, then amongst thousands that call themselves Christians."[80] Williams even portrayed aspects of Narragansett culture as ideals to be striven toward, confessing, "I have acknowledged amongst them an heart sensible of kindnesses, and have reaped kindnesse from many, seven years after, when I my selfe had forgotten, &c hence the Lord Jesus exhorts his followers to doe good for evill: for otherwise, sinners will do good for good, kindnesse for kindesse, &c.".[81]

Rhode Island itself was an anomaly in the colonial development of New England. Elsewhere, English encroachment had been effected through three means: seizure of unoccupied lands, legal purchase (under English rules and customs), and rights of conquest through 'just war'. In Rhode Island, the Narragansetts had officially welcomed and encouraged English settlement themselves. This model posed an implicit, yet potent challenge to Puritan legal assumptions. It also confronted the self-righteous attitudes of Puritans who saw themselves through the typological lens of Biblical history. Adding to the discomfort and embarrassment of comparisons, many of the new settlers in Rhode Island leveled a constant barrage of criticism and invective at the Puritans now surrounding them on all sides.

Obviously, having outspoken advocates for Native American rights on their doorstep did not serve the purposes of the Puritans to the north. On the other hand, Williams, along with others who chose the Rhode Island colony, continued to maintain a strong loyalty to England and to the neighboring English colonies. Williams' correspondence shows that he continued to play a key diplomatic role on behalf of all the New England colonies, helping often as an interpreter and intelligence gatherer until the last days of the King Philip War.

One of the more influential groups which fled to Rhode Island

---

[80] Ibid.17.
[81] Ibid 7-8

was led by non-conformist Samuel Gorton. Gorton's group was able to purchase land initially for a town on Narragansett territory in present day Pawtucket, although they removed to Warwick when Gorton was later arrested and jailed in Boston. One of the reasons for Gorton's influence was the trust and friendship which he had developed with the neighboring Narragansetts, in particular, the sachem Miantonomo. Eventually, Gorton's outspoken criticism of the Puritan colony to the north resulted in his arrest and deportation back to Massachusetts as well as the confiscation of his territory.

When the Puritan tactics used to depose the Gortonists were challenged back in England, the Massachusetts Bay government was pressured finally to free Gorton from prison and allow him to return to Rhode Island. Gorton's successful release at the request of the royal government in England astounded the Narragansetts, who were imminently concerned about both Plimoth and Massachusetts Bay encroachment and designs on their well cultivated territory. As a result, the Narragansetts determined that the best guarantee of their future autonomy would be to subject themselves to the King of England, thereby protecting themselves, like their friend Gorton, against future encroachment and domination by the Puritans. The following is Howard Chapins' description of the meeting of the coconspirators:

> Samuel Gorton, the founder of Warwick, who had been taken prisoner by Massachusetts soldiers, was released in 1644 and returned to Narragansett Bay. The Native Americans were greatly impressed by the fact that he had escaped with his life and sent for him to come and consult with them. Gorton, with some half dozen followers, crossed the bay by boat and was met by a "band of lusty, well armed men" and conducted to the house of Canonicus. After being entertained by the old sachem they were taken to the house of Pessacus and attended an Native American council. Gorton induced them, for their better protection against the Massachusetts men, to acknowledge themselves subjects of the English king. They thereupon drew up "The Act and Deed" of voluntary submission to King Charles, which was signed on April 19, 1644, by Pessacus as Chief Sa-

chem, by Canonicus as "Protector of the late deceased Miantonomi during the time of his nonage" and by Mixanno as son and heir of Canonicus.[82]

The next step was a tragic one for the Narragansetts. As soon as the submission was announced, the Narragansetts declared their intentions to proceed militarily against Uncas and the Mohegans. This declaration must have sent panic into the minds and hearts of the English, as both Plimoth and Massachusetts Bay immediately sent troops and an ultimatum to the Narragansetts to stop their war with the Mohegans. Capt. Myles Standish's troops from Plimoth were the first to arrive in Narragansett territory in August, marching directly into the heavily populated areas of Seekonk and Providence and terrifying the people who wondered if another massacre was intended. But Standish and the other English troops needed no introduction of their intent in this illegal violation of declared neutrality. The show of English force persuaded the Narragansett people and their leaders to back down.

Despite the good faith shown by the Narragansetts in honoring their treaties, Massachusetts Bay decided to punish the Narragansetts for the above incident by demanding an exorbitant payment of two thousand fathoms of white wampum for reparations caused by the incident. Additionally, Massachusetts Bay also demanded four children to serve as hostages in security for the payments. One of these was the oldest son of the Sachem, Pessacus, who had come to leadership with the murder of his father, Miantonomo. But the Narragansetts continued to honor their commitments, even under coercive pressures. It would require a preemptive attack by Puritans in the winter of 1675 to engage the tribe in overt hostilities. But it must have been clear to the Narragansetts that their future from this point on indeed was imperiled.

---

[82] Howard M. Chapin, <u>Sachems of the Narragansetts</u>, (Providence: Rhode Island Historical Society ,1931), 57-58.

Chapter 5
Religious Imperialism

On the heels of the Puritan expansion across southern New England, a public relations problem for the new colonies began to grow in England. Native Americans, settlers, and travelers in the Puritan colonies had been jailed, executed, or otherwise disciplined, and many had begun to raise their voices in protest. The voices were heard, particularly by members of Parliament. So, at the very time the Puritans had achieved dominance over the expanded territories, their experiment appeared to be jeopardized politically. Some of the criticism was scathing. Chief among the complaints was that all of the colonies had in some way violated English law. Most importantly, the Massachusetts Bay colony had violated its patent, first by sponsoring the Connecticut settlements, and then by co-sponsoring an unauthorized war against the Pequots. Connecticut also was vulnerable to legal challenges that would, over time, be exacerbated by the Dutch and English War. Under Edmund Andross, the New York colony would attempt, during the King Philip War, to assert a counterclaim against lands west of the Connecticut River held by the Hartford, New Haven, and New London governments.

Plimoth was perhaps in the best position of all the colonies to retain its territorial claims and proprietary interests. Plimoth had established itself and managed to expand its colony through purchase and other forms of legal encroachment against the surrounded Wampanoags. In addition, Plimoth, through its initial treaties with Wampanoag sachems, was given a charter as a protector of the Wampanoags.

Rhode Island, as a non-Puritan colony, was also not chartered at first, but, as more English nonconformists moved to the region, the settlements proceeded to gain the approval of the English Parliament. Unlike the Puritans of Massachusetts Bay and Connecticut, many nonconformists of Rhode Island willingly complied with English authority, and gained influence with prominent English political leaders as a result. Furthermore, the Narragansett tribes' submission to the English government extended a cloak of protection extending to English residents of the colony. From the perspectives of Rhode Island settlers, their good relations with the neighboring Narragansetts served their own interests as well, a legacy of Roger Williams' tireless diplomacy and efforts on behalf of both.

Massachusetts Bay had also come under criticism by those who had returned to England after being criminally prosecuted inside the colony. One of these was Samuel Maverick, one of the early planters who settled in Massachusetts Bay before the Puritan onrush. Maverick, who settled under the royal patent extended to Sir Ferdinando Gorges, principal of the New England Company, had a reputation as a libertine and had given refuge to various persons who had run afoul of the Puritan magistrates. Winthrop writes in 1641, "Another case fell out about Mr. Maverick of Nottles Island, who had been formerly fined L100 for giving entertainment to Mr. Owen and one Hale's wife, who had escaped out of prison, where they had been put out for notorious suspicion of adultery, as shall after be showed."[83] Maverick eventually was pressured to leave the colony, only to return again in 1664 as part of a joint commission sent from England to evaluate and recommend changes in Massachusetts Bay government.

While the Puritans were trying to control the political damage in England resulting from their internal conflicts, other critics were raising the question of missionary activity in New England, or rather the lack thereof. With the horrific spectacle of the Pequot War in the background, it became glaringly evident to Puritan critics that the Puritan migrations had been disastrous to Native Americans in New England. The Puritans claimed their presence in New England would carry spiritual benefits to Native Americans. Winthrop had stated in his original mandate for the new settlement, that iIt will be a service to the church of great consequence to carry the Gospell into those parts of the world."[84] In reality, however, Puritan efforts were almost completely lacking even as late as 1650 with two notable exceptions, and those were both outside Puritan jurisdiction on Cape Cod and Martha's Vineyard, where independent missions were successfully established by Thomas Mayhew and Richard Bourne. In Massachusetts Bay, however, the task of bringing the gospel to the Native Americans

---

[83] John Winthrop, <u>Winthrop's Journal</u>, (New York: Charles Scribner's Sons 1908), 47.

[84] John Winthrop, "Undated Paper", in <u>Life and Letters of John Winthrop</u>, 1588-1630, (Boston: Tecknor and Fields, 1864), 309.

Religious Imperialism and Cultural Genocide

had largely been passed over or ignored.

Furthermore, the delay and failure of Massachusetts Bay to establish an effective mission was criticized by other Puritans living abroad. Ray Jennings describes a dispute between the Puritan Congregationalists with English Presbyterians. He relates, "In a period of intense competition between English Presbyterians and Puritan Congregationalists, the Reverend Robert Baylie made a propaganda point with his condemnation of the Puritan's New England brethren, accusing them "of all that ever crossed the American Seas, are noted as most neglectful of the work of Conversion."[85]

The criticisms had a corrosive effect, and soon efforts were joined to answer the critics. In 1647, a lengthy tract, "The Day-Breaking If Not the Sun-Rising of the Gospell", was published as a defense to allay criticism. The format is reminiscent of many of John Eliot's writings, being presented in a form of questions and answers told from the perspective and memory of the English. What makes it particularly interesting is that it provided an elaborate theological rationale for the failure of Puritan missions to gain substantial number of converts. Below is a sample from the tract:

> We are upbraided by some of our Countrymen that so little good is done by our professing planters upon the hearts of Natives; such men have surely more splene than judgment, and know not the vast distance of Natives from common civility, almost humanity it selfe, and tis as if they should reproach us for not making the windes to blow when wee lift ourselves, it must certainly be a spirit of life from God (not in man's power) which must put flesh and sinewes unto these dry bones; if wee would force them to baptisme (as the Spaniards do about Cusco, Peru, and Mexico, having learnt them a short answer or two to some Popish questions) or if we would hire them to it by giving them coates and shirts, to allure them to it (as some others have done,) wee could have gathered many hundreds, yea thousands it may bee

---

85 Jennings, The Invasion of America, 236.

> by this time, into the name of churches; but wee have not learnt as yet that art of coyning Christians, or putting Christs name and Image upon copper mettle. Although I thinke we have much cause to bee humbled that wee have not endeavoured more than wee have done their conversion and peace with God, who enjoy the mercy and peace of God in their land. Three things have made us thinke (as they once did of building the Temple) it is not yet time for God to worke, 1. because till the Jewes come in, there is a seale set upon the hearts of those people, as they thinke from some Apocalyticall places. 2. That as in nature there is no progresse ab extreme ad extremum nifi per media, so in religion such are so extremely degenerate, must bee brought to some civility before religion can prosper, or the word take place. 3 Because we want miraculous and extraordinary gifts without which no conversion can bee expected amongst these; but me thinkes now that it is with the Native Americans as was with our New-English ground when we first came over, there was scarce any man that could beleeve that English graine would grow, or that the Plow could doe any good in this woody and rocky soile.[86]

Although this tract reflects the Puritan theological beliefs concerning the preparation required for conversion, it does not address the lack of effort in that regard. What it does demonstrate is that the Bay colony had taken its many critics seriously enough to answer them formally. It would be a major omission, in this regard, not to mention Roger Williams again. Williams, as evidence shows, was fervent and direct in his efforts to challenge Puritan ideas on a wide range of issues. On the issue of proselytizing, however, he took a contradictory position by damning Massachusetts Bay for not proselytizing, and then opposing them when they finally undertook an effort. Williams likely

---

86 John Eliot, The Day-Breaking If Not The Sun-Rising of the Gospell With the Indians in New-England (London: Printed by Rich. Cotes, for Fulk Clifton, 1647), 17.

Religious Imperialism and Cultural Genocide

had a more personal agenda in mind as well, which went far beyond the issue of Native American affairs, wanting to expose what he perceived to be Puritan hypocrisy in their persecution of heretics. In this regard, he was obviously struck by the inconsistency of the Puritans, comparing and contrasting their tolerance of native religious practices against their intolerance of English diversity. He writes, "I answer, that in New England it is well known that they not onely permit the Native Americans to continue in their unbeliefe, (which neither they, nor all the Ministers of Christ on Earth, nor Angels in Heaven can helpe, not being able to worke beleefe) but they also permit or tolerate them in their Paganish worship which cannot be denied to be a worshipping of Devils, as all false Worship is."[87]

Of course, Williams was wrong about Puritan tolerance of Native American religion. Williams was addressing an apparent double standard, but there were other reasons behind Puritan tolerance of the Massachusetts. Most important, the Puritans did not perceive the remnant villages of the once powerful Massachusett tribe as a threat to the colony, and indeed many Massachusett men had been helpful to the Puritan army during the Pequot War, serving as scouts and warriors. Thus, there was not enough pressure upon Massachusetts Bay to warrant the expenditure of funds to establish a mission, and the Puritan leaders were temporarily willing to accept the status quo. Williams was accurate in exposing the contradiction, but wrong in his interpretation.

Historians have treated Williams a bit too kindly, casting him as a staunch defender of Native Americans. That ignores the full scope of his words and actions. In portraying the worship of his Native American neighbors in such brutally negative terms, Williams appeared to be reflecting the opinion of most Puritan leaders of his day. English conceptions and interpretations of Native American spiritual beliefs in the seventeenth century were almost exclusively derived from European conceptions of witchcraft. But Williams, in raising the mission issue, was not suggesting that efforts to proselytize should be taken. In fact, he unambiguously opposed proselytizing Native Americans, as demon-

---

[87] Roger Williams, "The Bloudy Tenant of Persecution", in The Complete Writings of Roger Williams, vol. III, Samuel L. Caldwell, ed. (Providence, RI: Publications of the Narragansett Club,1867) 196-197.

strated in his own reluctance to proselytize despite every opportunity to do so, even though he clearly sent mixed signals on this matter when he was in England. Whether or not he ended up reversing his earlier stated position, he was unambiguously clear in his determination that attempts at proselytizing would end up in failure. The following portion from a letter on this issue, written by Williams to Winthrop, reveals the rather contradictory viewpoint of the exiled Puritan:

> Sir I hope shortly to send you good newes of great hopes the Lord hath sprung up in mine Eye of many a poore Native American soule enquiring after God. I have convinced hundreths at home and abroad that in point of Religion they are all wandring etc. I find what I could never heare before, that they have plenty of Gods or divine powers: the Sunn, Moone, Fire, Water, Snow, Earth, the Deere, the Beare etc. are divine powers. I brought home lately from the Nanhiggonsicks the names of 38 of their Gods all they could remember and had I not with feare and caution withdrew they would have fallen to worship O God (as they speake one day in 7). [88]

In hesitating to work toward the conversion of his Narragansett neighbors, Williams was obviously concerned about their lack of preparation and spiritual understanding to take on Christian beliefs. He knew that, in reality, Native American cosmologies could easily accommodate many features of Christianity, but for him it was not enough. The willingness of Native Americans to follow English ways and adopt religious beliefs without discarding their own ways was famously depicted in the writings of John Eliot as well. They were willing to add the Christian god to their already crowded pantheon, but unwilling to push any others out. But this was far less than Puritan leaders demanded of English settlers, and Williams was astute enough to point it out, with embarrassing effects in England. In effect, Williams had drawn a line with his argument, reinforcing an admonition that would later be given legal protection by his political allies in Parliament.

---

[88] Roger Williams, "Letter to John Winthrop dated 28 Feb., 1637", in The Complete Writings of Roger Williams, 146.

Religious Imperialism and Cultural Genocide

Williams' harsh criticism of the Puritans elicited a direct written response from John Cotton. Cotton had already penned a book defending the Puritans against the criticisms of Baillie in England, and taking on Williams in Rhode Island must have seemed even more necessary, given the rising tide of criticism and complaints, most of them from Rhode Island. Responding to Williams' allusion to the Narragansett's openness to Christianity, Cotton counterattacked with his own accusation of hypocrisy:

> ...Mr. [Roger] Williams his speech doth not so much hold forth the facility of the Native Americans to any such conversion, as might fit them for church estate, but rather the hypocrisy and formality of the ordinary church members of national churches; which he professeth is so far off from true conversion, that it is the subverion of the souls of many millions in Christendom, from one false worship to another.

> ...It is no unhappiness of any principle of ours, that hath kept Mr. Williams from making use of his great opportunity, and open door, to propogate the Gospel amongst the Native Americans. For though their facility to such a carnal conversion, as he describeth, gave him no just warrant, to gather them into a church estate; yet it was a just encouragement to provoke him (who understood their language) to have preached the Word of God unto them, which might have been mighty through God (if sincerely dispensed) to have turned them from darkness to light, from the power of Satan unto God, and so have prepared them, both for church fellowship here, and for heaven hereafter.

> ...But if Mr. [Robert[Baillie conceive that either Mr. Williams, or else we were to be blamed, because we do not presently receive Native Americans into the fellowship of our churches, seeing their facility to conform their outward man to us, and to so much of our religion, as Mr. Williams mentioned: he shall do

> well to consider beforehand, whether Jacob's children did well to persuade the Schechemites, Gen. XXXIV, to receive circumcision, before they better understood the covenant of Abraham (to which circumcision was a seal) and had made some better profession of taking hold of it.[89]

Eventually, when the Puritans did build a missionary program, it was as much in response to their own internal needs as it was to criticism from outside the colony. The men they would select for the enterprise, John Eliot and Daniel Gookin, were both enthusiastic and committed to the cause, and dedicated to the general welfare of Native Americans. Nevertheless, Puritan proselytizing overseen by Eliot would eventually prove to be fatal to native cultural autonomy, mainly because Eliot saw the necessity of challenging indigenous authority, in particular sachems and shamans (pauwaus), in order to undermine the structure of Algonquin society. This would reveal itself through the strenuous objections of Algonquin leaders and people to the first Puritan missionary activities overseen by John Eliot and Gookin, whose role as a magistrate for Native American Affairs under the Massachusetts Bay government would have profound effects upon the Native Americans.

Together, Eliot and Gookin grasped upon a solution to the dilemma facing the Puritans. Instead of confining the mission's activities to preaching and teaching, they proposed to consolidate the various Native American villages in Massachusetts into "praying townes" where they would be subjected to Puritan religious teachings and English laws. In the Puritan Commonwealth, that meant conformity with English customs, language, economic practices, work, and religious practices. Massachusetts Bay colony also managed to reach beyond the bounds of its own patent into Rhode Island. By pressuring two Narragansett sachems, Pomham and Sacononoco of Pawtuxet and Shawomet to submit to the authority of Massachusetts Bay, a legal means of interfering in the affairs of Rhode Island was created. In the end, the Puritan government was able to manipulate the situation, thus extending their

---

[89] John Cotton, "The Way of Congregational Churches Cleared", in John Cotton on the Churches of New England, Larzer Ziff, ed. (Cambridge: The Belknap Press, 1968), 268-279.

Religious Imperialism and Cultural Genocide

legal jurisdiction into Rhode Island and, just as importantly, gain legal authority to arrest Samuel Gorton, a man who had continued to wage a campaign against the Puritan government, and whose influence among Rhode Island dissenters was growing rapidly.

Interestingly, in March of 1644, three Massachusett sachems declared their submission to the Massachusetts General Court, actions that have been the subject of controversy among scholars in the field. The sachems included the Squaw Sachem, Cutshamequin and Masconomono, the last remaining leaders of the remnant Massachusett tribe residing in the Boston area. Following their submissions, others followed in suit, including Native Americans from the north and west of Boston, including a legendary leader named Passconoway, who served as both sachem and pauwau with his people. While some, including prominent scholar Ray Salisbury, have argued that the reasons for the submissions were fear that they would receive the same fate as Miantonomo, who had been executed. It is also possible they had different motives. Richard Cokley suggests it was fear of the Narragansetts that sparked the submissions, writing, "Jennings is probably right that the execution of Maintonomi terrified the Massachusetts and Pawtuckets, and probably wrong wabout the reason for their alarm, they feared the Narragansetts, not the saints (Puritans)."[90] Cokley's inference is certainly consistent with previous declarations, basically showing the Native Americans inexorably linked with their English masters, setting them at odds with other Native Americans.

Even with the submissions, Puritan leaders were aware that more efforts would be required to bring Native Americans into conformity with the Puritan way of life. Though the terms of submission required certain accommodations and Native American tolerance of Puritan rules and customs, it is abundantly clear that the Massachusett Native Americans were unable to force their people to fully comply. Thus, the subjection of the sachems represents a solution to the inconsistency, while prosecuting English nonconformity. But even with these good faith efforts, Native American willingness to adapt to English ways was never enough. Puritan leaders knew that a more robust effort to bring Native Americans into the Puritan mainstream would be required.

---

[90] Cogley, Richard W, John Eliot Mission to the Indians Before King Philip's War, 35

Hidden Genocide, Hidden People

It was John Eliot, the minister of the Roxbury church, who would rise to the occasion, and organize a mission to convert the Native Americans in Puritan-controlled territories. After having studied the Algonquin language for about five years, Eliot publicly began his mission with a failed preaching mission to a Massachusett town at Dorchester Mills led by the sachem Cutshamiquin in July, 1646. Cutshamequin was a well-known figure to Massachusetts Bay settlers, and played a key role as an emissary and ally, though his relations with the Puritans were punctuated with disagreements and tensions. It was reported that Eliot was badly heckled at that meeting, no doubt a result of Cutshamequin's own reticence, a fact that renders his earlier submission rather moot in importance. Right away, Eliot became aware of the staunch resistance he was facing, and the need for a more comprehensive approach, consistent with Puritan beliefs that extensive preparation and evidence of personal conversion were required for church membership.

As a pastor whose instincts were honed in ministering to the personal needs and of his congregation, Eliot knew that he was speaking to a deeply-humiliated and long-suffering people who had every reason to resent the English religion. The Massachusett tribal villages had been squeezed on all sides in the Boston area, and their traditional means of survival had been greatly hampered by the English farms and towns spreading out rapidly west and north from its center in Massachusetts. Eliot must have known immediately that another approach would be needed in order to succeed in his mission, beginning with a legal re-ordering of Native American communities into what would become known as "praying townes". It took people like Eliot to bolster this sense of confidence in the new future his mission would eventually bring, but a major obstacle remained in convincing Native Americans that they should shun their leaders and traditions and embrace the Puritan way.

Although a Puritan, Eliot's ideas were based on an interpretation of the millenium radically different from that of other Puritan clergy. Instead of the Puritans at the center of a great revival, Eliot placed the Native Americans at the center instead. Here, one is tempted to see him as extreme in his viewpoints, but his attitudes, gentle demeanor and affection toward Native Americans was something different altogether, and reaffirmed his beliefs. While Eliot did not hesitate to de-

Religious Imperialism and Cultural Genocide

mean Native American spiritual practices and governance, he esteemed them in many other ways, recognizing the humanistic principles and values which guided their way, while extolling the character of many individuals he knew. To Eliot, Christianity would refine these characteristics, and exalt Native Americans into the vanguard of a worldwide movement toward a more true and refined Christian church. Eliot saw his mission as critical to that movement, seeing the Native Americans as heralding the second phase of the millenium in preparation for the final return of Christ in glory. Before that could happen, however, the Native Americans would have to be converted, and the church and civil order restored to a state consistent with the directives of scripture. However, it was not to be a typical conversion, but one which would be guided solely by scriptural principles, as interpreted by Eliot himself.

Eliot's theology inferred a very special role for the Native Americans who lived around Massachusetts. While some, if not most Puritan religious leaders taught that the Native Americans were descended from ancient Tartars who managed to reach America in the distant past, a theory which implied that they were Gentiles by blood, Eliot took another popular view of their origins, namely that they were Jews. This was not an unpopular view in his day among many non-Puritan English, having been promoted and taught by a Presbyterian minister from Scotland, Rev. Thomas Thorowgood, the leading advocate for the theory in that day. Eliot had corresponded with Throrwgood in a lengthy letter, and it is clear that Thorowgood's theories provided the underlying theological rationale for Eliot's mission to the Native Americans. It was a simple formula which shifted the entire theological structure of New England Puritanism, mainly because of the high level of importance placed upon their successful conversion to Christianity. Throwgood explains it quite simply in his well known pamphlet, published with the title, *Jews in America*. He writes, "The people that have not yet received the Gospell of Jesus Christ are Jewes, but the Americans have not yet been gospelized; and here three things come to consideration. All other nations at first received the Gospell. The Jews before the end of the world shall be converted. These Native Americans have not yet heard of Christ."[91]

The theory that Native Americans had Jewish origins was a

---

[91] Thorowgood, Thomas, Jews in America, (London, 1660), 20

common belief in the 16th century, and while he is often credited as the major source of the theory, Thorowgood's ideas were borrowed by John Eliot. Eliot incorporated the theory into his rationale for the mission, arguing that its success would trigger a world-wide revival of a perfected form of Christianity. In order achieve that lofty goal, he determined he'd have to eliminate the influence of the pauwaus and sachems by reinserting a local governing model based on the laws of ancient Israel. In effect, the new community that he would create, scourged of its native beliefs and practices, would be a perfected version of even the existing Puritan towns.

Much of Eliot's thinking was merely a reflection of the times, partidularly in light of the civil war taking place in England. The temporary destruction of the monarchy and political chaos in England under Oliver Cromwell seems, indeed, to have actually inspired him to think in majestic categories, taking the social, religious and political upheaval taking place as a sign of the impending millenium. Here, there is much that could be concluded about Eliot's psychological state, having projected himself into the very center of a world-wide religious reformation. Grandiose thinking of this magnitude actually seems to have been the norm among many Puritan clergy in New England, but only Eliot himself was willing to put his claim to the test. If the mission succeeded, it would be to his eternal credit. But the only way it could succeed was through the preservation of Native Americans in New England. In becoming their spiritual leader, Eliot would also be compelled to be their protector, a role which would trigger tragically ironic results, hastening their demise rather than the opposite. Thus in the ensuing years, we find Eliot unwittingly and ironically fanning the flames of antagonism which eventually led to the genocidal King Philip War.

Eliot's plan included the revamping of Native American governments through the impostion of the biblical laws of ancient Jews, whom he believed were the ancestors of the New England Native Americans, having descended from Noah's son Shem. Richard Cogley describes how this new biblically based government was to be structured:

> The Apostle anticipated that once they were installed in power, the rulers of tens, fifties, and hundreds would preserve the other two institutional

Religious Imperialism and Cultural Genocide

components of the millenium. The first was the ecclesiastical polity. Although he changed his mind about the matter after the Restoration, he believed during the Interregnum that Congregationalism was the millennial church order. The second was the judicial laws of Moses "in so far as they are moral and conscionable." Eliot's commitment to the restitution of ancient Israelite law sometimes reached such proportions that it seeming entailed the total eradication of all man-made legal systems, including those in England.[92]

Eliot's theories seem to have made sense to some local Native Americans, many of whom saw an opportunity to gain status and position under the English system. Even sachems like Cutshamequin, who had in earlier years castigated the preaching of Eliot, eventually acquiesced along with others around the Boston region. Others such as Waban, the celebrated leader of first gathered community in Nonantum, appeared to have grasped the new government as an opportunity to ascend to positions of power and prestige in their community formerly given only to sachems and pauwaus.

One wonders why Native Americans were so malleable in regards the "praying townes" and the strict codes of behavior imposed upon the residents. Here, it is important to note that the Native Americans of New England did not have the elaborate legal and governing mechanisms of European societies, a trait which actually enabled them to thrive in New England for several thousand years. When they first encountered Europeans, they were basically left in the dark about the complex legal traditions, governance and policy-making processes in European societies. Of course, by the 1640's, they had already become entwined in the English legal system, much to their detriment. To them, Eliot's system seemed simpler and more malleable, avoiding the complexities of English traditions and law, while allowing for a local indigenous control. Rules and laws would be simple and enforced by local leaders, and governance would be according to patterns set in the Bible for the ancient Hebrews.

Eliot believed that Native Americans could enter fully into Eng-

---

[92] Coagley, Richard, <u>John Eliot's Mission to the Indians before King Philip's War</u>, Harvard University Press, (Cambridge, MA 1999), 78

Hidden Genocide, Hidden People

lish economic activities, and become farmers like the English settlers. Above all, Eliot's blueprint required a full transformation of native culture to an exacting English way of life. This required more than a little adjustment in native expectations and social mores, something which Eliot appears to have not foreseen. Among Native Americans, trade was a traditional means of maintaining social stability and enhancing cooperation. In English society, trade was typically more aggressive, creating a system of winners and losers. This was not the way of Algonquin people and culture, who saw natural resources as a common pot from which all could draw.

In English society, the wealthy and powerful harnessed resources and land unto themselves by exploiting the labors of others in the process. In Algonquin society, as testified by countless European settlers and explorers in contrast, wealth was essentially a transient quality, and had little or nothing to do with exploitation of other human beings. This is why the Wampanoags extended initial friendliness and outreach to the Pilgrims, expecting reciprocity rather than competition for resources and land. The custom in Algonquin cultures asserted the sachem/sagamore as the leader of the community, and in this role had responsibility for the management of community resources, especially land, ensuring the collective well-being of the people. There was, in effect, no true sense of ownership of land, and when disputes did take place, sachems typically called together councils to discuss and decide matters of importance. Lisa Brooks, in her excellent book, The Common Pot, cogently explains these important characteristics of Native American culture, elements of which could never truly be compatible with the European model about to be imposed upon Eliot's Native Americans in 1644. She writes:

> Inherent in the concept of the common pot is the idea that whatever was given from the larger network of inhabitants had to be shared within the human community. ...If one person went hungry, if certain individuals were excluded from the bounty of the dish, the whole would face physical and/or psychological repercussions from this rupture in the network of relations.[93]

---

[93] Brooks, Lisa, The Common Pot, University of Minnesota Press, 2008, 5

Eliot was both keenly aware of the qualities and characteristics of native culture described by Brooks. First, willingness to share resources was documented not only by Eliot, but by countless other English explorers and writers, including Puritans. Indeed, it is the memory of Native American generosity itself which informs the Thanksgiving celebration in the United States. But another just important, although often overlooked characteristic of Algonquin culture was the importance placed upon honesty and trust. This impressed many English writers, particularly non-Puritans such as Samuel Gorton, Roger Williams and Thomas Morton, and many more who affirmed the integrity of Native American leaders and the open and balanced approach they took in making decisions. Even Puritans sometimes reflected respect in the way Algonquin leaders conducted their affairs. Edward Johnson, a writer who normally disdained Native American culture, even admired the way in which the Narragansetts carefully considered their participation in the Pequot War:

> In this place sate their Sachim, with very great attendance; the English comming to deliver their Message, to manifest the greater state, the Native American Sachim lay along upon the ground on a Mat, and his Nobility sate on the ground, with their legs doubled up, their knees touching their chin; with much sober gravity they attend the Interpreters speech. It was matter of much wonderment to the english, to see how solidly and wisely these savage people did consider of the weighty undertaking of a War; especially old Canonicus, who was very discreet in his answers.[94]

In typical Algonquin villages, Sachems/Sagamores were empowered by their people to negotiate with outsiders and speak on their behalf, providing a means of collective identity and social cohesion. One example is in terms of proprietary rights over territory. The sachem (or sagamore) was responsible for apportioning out lands as needed to tribal members, a commodity that was in great overabundance in Massachusetts following the great epidemic. By 1644, however, land

---

[94] Johnson, Wonder-Working Providence, 162

had become increasingly scarce. But even with diminished numbers, the Massachusetts were in danger of being squeezed out of the region. This fact probably had much to do with the submission of the sachems, assuming they saw that submission as a guarantor of their legal rights to their land. With a rapidly transforming economy forcing Native Americans into cash crops and husbandry, survival required adaptation. Cutshamequin understood this need, but he also was capable of discerning the implications of Puritan plans to convert his people to Christianity, especially in terms of undermining his own authority, and on this matter he was determined to resist.

Resistance and outright hostility to the Puritan religion among other Algonquin leaders and people was painfully evident to Eliot. The rejection at Dorchester Mill by Cutshamiquin's people convinced Eliot that, in order to make progress at other villages, he would have to eliminate the pauwaus and sachems/sagamores. From Eliot's point of view, it was native spirituality and the role of pauwaus that was the binding force within Algonquin communities. Eliot was also astute enough to acknowledge the legitimacy of some of the healing methods used by pauwaus. Otherwise, he deemed them in league with the devil, as did most Puritans. Thus Eliot made little progress in effecting conversions until he took a more comprehensive approach designed to undermine tribal structures and authority. Concentrating his efforts on a small village at Nonantum (Newton), Eliot established what would become the first "praying townes" in Massachusetts. Selecting a recent convert from Nonantum named Waban, Eliot appointed him to a newly created position as Chief Minister of Justice over the town, giving him a legal leadership status in the eyes of English law. In turn, those who would come to occupy the "Praying Towns" would be required to follow English laws, including those which specifically forbade Native religious practices. Eliot believed such steps were necessary to bring Native Americans into an advanced state of civilization. Ironically, the move dismantled tribal structures and practices which extended back thousands of years in time. Thus, it is a misnomer to refer to Native Americans as primitive, as Eliot's rhetoric suggests. Politically and culturally, the Europeans were but 'babes in the woods' in comparison to Algonquins and most other American Native American tribes as well, but this was not evident to Eliot, a believer in the primacy of Christianity over all else.

Nevertheless, despite the deep differences between the European and Native American civilizations, Eliot's plan worked. The reason is that the long term success of these tribal customs and structures had allowed for a zone of vulnerability, and Eliot knew how to exploit it. Lacking the sophisticated and vast legal and governmental apparatus associated with European governments, the Algonquin cultural meanings and behaviors were derived from the ancient stories, legends, and lessons from the past. Within this ancient order and tradition stood the sachem and the pauwau (shaman), leadership roles with deep roots in archaic societies worldwide. The pauwau (shaman) was responsible mainly for healing functions, both physical and psychic, within the community. But the pauwaus were also believed to have extraordinary supernatural powers which the English equated with devil worship and witchcraft. Henry Bowden and James Ronda describe this aspect of the pauwau's role:

> Pauwaus flourished in almost every village, and they served in varied ways including dream interpretation, curing, predicting the future, and acting as intermediaries between human an spiritual levels of the integrated cosmos. Natives believed shamans were capable of entering trances wherein their souls left the mundane sphere to commune with spirit beings. Once they revived or became whole again, they relayed special messages from divine powers to designated individuals or to the entire group.[95]

Eliot obviously thought it would be impossible to convince the sachems to disenfranchise the pauwaus, and he noted this in several different letters and tracts. Instead, with the onset of mission activity, at the behest of Eliot and Gookin, the influence and role of the pauwaus and sachems was dealt with by the General Court by an enactment prohibiting the practice of native religion in its territory in 1646. This action had the effect of instantly severing the religious, organizational,

---

[95] Henry W. Bowden and James P. Ronda, ed., John Eliot's Indian Dialogues, A Study in Cultural Interaction, (Westport, CT: Greenwood Press, 1980), 13.

Hidden Genocide, Hidden People

and ancestral links which had provided order and meaning to Algonquin society for so many millenia. At the same time, the Massachusetts Bay General Court authorized the creation of a praying towne to be called "Nonantum" with the following mandate: "for the honor of the eternall God, whom only we worship and serve, that no person within the jurisdiction, whether Christian or pagan, shall wittingly and willingly presume to blaspheme his holy name, either by wilfull or obstinate denying the true God, or his creation or government of the world, or shall curse God or reproach the holy religion of God... if any person or persons whatsoever, within our jurisdiction whatsoever, shall break this lawe shall be put to death."[96] This was an insidious requirement for the non-Christians in the village, for it implied the penalty of death for the practice of any native religious or cultural customs, depending upon the whims of English interpretations and sensitivities. No occupant would certainly want to cross Eliot or any of his informants by seeming disrespectful or discourteous during church services, considering the dire consequences.

One of the more subtle ironies in the establishment of the "praying town" of Nonantum was the fact that the land upon which it was established was purchased by the General Court and then apportioned out to the residents. This also violated traditional Algonquin practice wherein the Sachem was the titular holder of lands, and the concept of the English purchasing land for dispossessed Native Americans must have appeared strange and quite threatening to other Native Americans. But the real irony in this affair is the fact that many English settlers criticized the deal for being biased for the Native Americans. Daniel Gookin must have felt this criticism was important enough to respond to from the outset:

> If any should object, that it is not necessary, that the English should grant them land, forasmuch as it was all their native country and propriety, before the English came into America; the answer is ready: First, that the English claim right to their land, by patent from our king. Secondly, yet the English had the grant of most of the land within this jurisdiction, either

---

[96] Jennings, <u>Invasion of America</u>, 240.

Religious Imperialism and Cultural Genocide

> by purchase or donation from the Native American sachems and sagamores, which were actually in possession, when the English came first over. Therefore the propriety is in the English; and it is necessary for the Native Americans, as the case stands, for their present and future security and tranquility, to receive the lands by grant from the English, who are a growing and potent people, comparatively to the Native Americans.[97]

While Eliot's intent may have been to nurture the formation of Puritan religion, his strategy involved undermining Algonquin customs and laws, and replacing them with English ones. This changeover would be complete, even down to the creation of laws passed by the converted Native Americans under Eliot's oversight. These laws were intended for the entire community, especially because so few Native Americans actually converted to Christianity. Below is a set of the first laws established for Nonantum, along with an editorial notes in parenthesis by the author, Eliot:

> Wee have cause to be very thankfull to God who hath moved the hearts of the generall court to purchase so much land for them to make their towne in which the Native Americans are much taken with, and it is somewhat observable that while the Court were considering [p.28] where to lay out their towne, the Native Americans (not knowing of any thing) were about that time consulting about Lawes for themselves, and there company who sit downe with Waaubon; there were ten of them, two of them are forgotten. Their Lawes were these.
>
> 1. That if any man be idle a weeke, at most a fortnight, hee shall pay five shillings.
> 2. If any unmarried man shall lie with a young woman unmarried, he shall pay twenty shillings.
> 3. If anyman shall beat his wife, his hands shall bee

[97] Daniel Gookin, <u>Historical Collections of the Indians In New England,</u> (London, 1677), 62-63.

tied behind him and carried to the place of justice to bee severely punished.

4. Every young man if not anothers servant, and if unmarried, hee shall be compelled to set up a Wigwam and plan for himselfe, and not live shifting up and downe to other Wigwams.

5. If any woman shall not have her haire tied up but hang loose or be cut as mens haire, shee shall pay five shillings.

6. if any woman shall goe with naked breasts they shall pay two shillings sixpence.

7. All those men that weare long locks shall pay five shillings.

8. If any shall kill their lice betweene their teeth, they shall pay five shillings. This Law though ridiculous to English eares yet tends to preserve cleanliness among Native Americans.[98]

Through the organizing effort of Eliot and Daniel Gookin, a deputy of the General Court of Massachusetts Bay and a man who was sympathetic to Native Americans, local governments were established in "praying townes"; the purpose of the towns was to bring the tribes into conformity with Puritan laws and customs. Without the opposition of tribal leaders and the continuation of ancestral traditions, the Massachusetts Native Americans became even more susceptible to Puritan influence with this major structural change. The praying towns brought other radical changes to the Algonquin way of life as well. First, the concept of permanent dwellings and private property was an alien one to the Massachusetts. Secondly, the transition to private farms involved the physical separation of family groups and clans. Traditionally, much of the food production were both collective and non competitive activities, with women taking responsibility for planting and maintaining crops. Under the Puritan system, men took the place of women in the fields, and women were encouraged to engage in more domestic types of activities, such as spinning and weaving. Tradition-

---

[98] Eliot, <u>The Day-Breaking If Not The Sun-Rising of the Gospell With the Indians in New-England,</u> 29-29.

Religious Imperialism and Cultural Genocide

ally, during fishing season, groups from various villages would gather together for joint fishing activities. These enterprises were not just economic in nature; they also helped to reaffirm the ties between families and clans. Hence, the Algonquin people made these harvests a means of community affirmation and celebration through annual games and feasts. With the organization of the remnants of this tribe into praying towns, these ancient customs began to rapidly disappear.

The "praying town" eventually became the normative arrangement for hundreds of Massachusetts. In addition, Puritan expansion into inland areas adjacent to Penacooks, Nipmucs and others brought them into control of virtually all of southern New England, hastening the process of relocating Native Americans into "praying townes". By 1660, there would be ten "praying townes", based upon the Nonantum pattern. The number eventually grew to fourteen by the King Philip War. Despite the rapid growth, however, the number of Native Americans actually converted in the "praying townes" remained low, so low, in fact, that the first truly autonomous Native American congregation wasn't formed until 1660 in Natick, where most of the original community of Nonatum was resettled in 1651.

One of the reasons for the relative success of Eliot's strategy, aside from theological imperatives, was the strong financial support the missions received from England. Indeed, the enterprise was a rather lucrative one for the colonies as donations not only supported Eliot's mission, but also provided for the establishment of an Native American Department at Harvard College with a substantial amount left to purchase weapons for the colony. The financial undergirding allowed for an ambitious program of outreach and the underwriting expenses associated with the various publications put out by Eliot. Some of these were catechetical aids, but a substantial amount of effort also went into the publication of tracts and other publications for English consumption.

While the "praying towns" demonstrated the efficacy of Puritan management of Native American affairs, baptisms and actual conversions were fairly rare. Therefore, Eliot, in his correspondence to the Society for the Propagation of the Gospel in England, was prone to "padding" his reports. One way Eliot accomplished by implying that Thomas Mayhew Jr.'s and Richard Bourne's successful missions on Cape Cod and Martha's Vineyard were a connected to his own. Eliot further used another deceptive tactic by stating that the Native Americans on Cape Cod and Martha's Vineyard were related to the Massachusett sachem, Cutshamaquin, implying that the relationship conferred a further connection between Eliot and Mayhew's activities. Eliot was obviously 'pulling the wool over the eyes' of his patrons. Going even further, in his 1660 report, rather than start with a report on the "praying towns" of Massachusetts, he refers the Commissioners of the Society to Mayhew and Bourn. He writes, "That brief Tract of the present state of the Native American Work in my hand, which I did the last year on the sudden present you with when you call'd for such a thing; That falling short of its end, and you calling for a renewal thereof, with opportunity of more time, I shall begin with our last great motion in the Work done the Summer, because that will lead me to begin with the state of the Native Americans under the hands of my Brethren Mr. Mahew and Mr. Bourn."[99]

Eliot also attempted to engender support by publishing various books and tracts for public consumption, mainly back in England. One of the more interesting tracts is *Native American Dialogues*, originally published in 1671. It contains lengthy dialogues between various Native American missionaries and their audiences and kinfolk. While the dialogues are presented as verbatim reports, they were probably embellished by Eliot, something that is obvious by the consistent syntax and distinctly English idiomatic expresssions within the text. Nevertheless, they provide a wealth of insight into the English perception of native culture, and also a glimpse of the attitudes and responses of various Native Americans to the proselytizing efforts of Puritan missionaries.

Initially, proselytizing was conducted mainly among the Massachusetts, Penacooks, and Nipmucs, but eventually Eliot sought to extend the mission to the Wampanoags and the Narragansetts. His strategy was to use converts selected out of the "praying towns" for preaching, teaching, and personal witness to the autonomous tribes, but these efforts met with stubborn opposition; Eliot did not hide this, and actually portrayed it to demonstrate the superiority of Puritanism

---

[99] John Eliot, <u>A Brief Narrative of the Progress of the Gospel Among the Indians of New England</u>, (Boston: John K. Wiggin & Wm. Parsons Lunt, 1868), 19.

Religious Imperialism and Cultural Genocide

over Algonquin beliefs and practices. He accomplished this largely by portraying a harsh contrast of English and Native American culture, portraying the Native Americans as agents of evil and corruption.

The Native American missionaries portrayed in Eliot's *Dialogues* appear unremitting in their efforts to win the souls of their neighbors, even to the point of exasperating them. Eliot recounts the travels and conversations of one of his missionaries, Piumbukhou, who was sent to a Nipmuc village near Windham, Ct.. Eliot portrays the missionary as being warmly and familiarly greeted by the villagers, among whom lived a cousin with whom he appears to have a close relationship. In the course of his visit, he initiates conversations with various Nipmucs, sharing with them his newfound religious faith, friendship with the English, and confronting them with his harsh judgments of tribal traditions. "Your joys are bodily, fleshly, such as dogs have, and will all turn to flames in hell to torment you.", he warns his family and friends.[100] While the dialogues are represented as friendly encounters, the audience find themselves confounded and exasperated with the missionary's persistence. Below are selected portions from the long series of dialogues. The first dialogue is between the Native American missionary, Piumbukho, a kinswoman and a small group of anonymous listeners:

> PIUM. The Book of God is no invention of Englishmen. It is the holy law of God himself, which was given unto man by God, before Englishmen had any knowledge of God; and all the knowledge which they have, they have it out of the Book of God. And this book is given to us as well as to them, and it is as free for us to search the scriptures as for them. …Yet this is also true, that we have great cause to be thankful to the English, and to thank god for them. For they had a good country of their own, but by ships sailing into these parts of the world, they heard of us, and of our country, and of our nakedness, ignorance of God, and wild condition. …They love us, they do us right, and no wrong willingly. If any do us wrong, it is without

---

[100] Eliot, <u>Indian Dialogues</u>, 71.

the consent of their rulers, and upon our complaints
our wrongs are righted. ...They are (many of them,
especially the ruling part) good men, and desire to
do us good. God put it into the heart of one of their
ministers (as you all know) to teach us the knowledge
of God, by the word of God, and hath translated the
holy Book of God into our language, so that we can
perfectly know the mind and counsel of God.

...KINSWOMAN. You make long and learned
discourses to us which we do not well understand. I
think our best answer is to stop your mouth, and fill
your belly with a good supper, and when your belly is
full you will be content to take rest yourself, and give
us leave to be at rest from these gastering and heart-
trembling discourses. We are well as we are, and desire
not to be troubled with these new wise sayings.[101]

Despite fervent pleadings and admonitions, the *Dialogues* never seem to effect the kind of conversions which the Puritans sought. Instead of openness, the Nipmuc responses remained resolute in opposition to Piumbukho's preaching. One of the more illustrative portions of the dialogues include an engagement between the missionary and the village pauwau, demonstrating the English conviction that Algonquin religious practices were devil worship. This portion begins with a stern rebuke by the pauwau against Piumbukho, the missionary:

PAUWAU. Let me add a few words to give check
to your high-flown confidence to your new way, and
new laws, and to your deep censoriousness of our old
ways, the pleasancey and delight whereof everyone,
both man, woman, and child, can judge of. And we
cannot but dislike to have such pleasant delights taken
from us. Tear our hair from our heads, our skin from
our flesh, our flesh from out bones, you shall as soon
persuade us to suffer you to do by us, as to persuade
us to part with our old delights and courses. You tell
us of the englishman's God, and of his laws. We have

---

[101] Ibid., 71-73.

Gods also, and more than they. And we have laws also by which our forefathers did walk, and why should we do as they have done? To change our gods, and laws, and customs, are great things, and not easily to be obtained and accomplished. Let us alone, that we may be quiet in the ways which we like and love, as we let you alone in your changes and new ways.

ALL. You say right. Why trouble they us in our pleasures and delights? Let us alone in our enjoyments.

PIUM. You have spoken many things, which do minister matter to me of much discourse, both concerning god, and our selves, and concerning you, and the offer of God's mercy to you at this time. You say you have many gods, but they are no gods. There is but one God, the great creator of this great world. did your gods make this world, the heavens, the sun, the moon, the stars, the clouds, the seas, and the whole earth? No, no. god made this whole world. Can any of your gods give rain, or rule the clouds? It is the Devil that blindeth your eyes, and God, who can kill us, or keep us alive at his pleasure. Your gods shall all perish with you, for they are no gods.

As for your pleasures and delights, they are all sins against God, which provoke his wrath to plague you forever. We now call you to repent of your evil ways, and to reform your lives to serve the true and living God, to seek for pardon of your sins, and mercy to appease his wrath which is kindled against you. I do now offer you mercy through Jesus Christ. Do not harden your hearts against the Lord. Be therefore persuaded now to forsake your sins and turn unto the Lord. Come unto the light out of your darkness. Awake from your dead sleep, stand up, and Christ will give you life. We speak by experience. We were dead and blind as you are. We loved pleasures as you do, but by the grace of Christ we have found light and life, and now call you to partake with us in our mercies.

PAUWAU. We have not only our pleasures, but also prayers and sacrifices. We beat and afflict our selves to pacify our Gods. And when we be sick we use such ways to recover our health, and to obtain all such things as we want, and desire to obtain from our Gods.

PIUM. Your prayers and pauwauings are worshipping of the Devil, and not of God, and they are among the greatest of your sins. Your murders, lusts, stealing, lying, etc., they are great sins. Your pauwauings are worse sins, because by them you worship the Devil instead of God. When you pauwaus use physic by roots, and such other things which God hath made for that purpose, that is no sin. You do well to use physic for your recovery from sickness. But your praying to, and worshipping the Devil, that is your great sin, which now God calls you to forsake. Use only such remedies as God hath appointed and pray to God. This we call you to do, and this is the way of true wisdom.[102]

In the course of the *Dialogues*, Eliot was obviously intent upon documenting the resistance of pauwaus, and the threat which they represented to his influence and authority. Of course, Eliot also used the Dialogues to portray the resistance of the sachems as well. One important encounter is recorded in the "Dialogues" between another Native American missionary named Anthony and Philip Keitasscot, also known as the legendary King Philip or Metacomet. Metacomet's response to the arguments of the missionary portrays the Sachem having a reasonable fear of the effects of missionization on his tribe, but nevertheless open and amicable to the Christian religion. He writes:

KEIT. (Philip) Often have I heard of this great matter of praying unto God, and hitherto I have refused. Mr. Eliot, Junior, while he was alive, attempted

---

[102] Eliot, "Dialogues", 87-89.

it, but I did not hearken unto his persuasion. Old Mr. Eliot himself did come unto me. He was in this town, and did persuade me. But we were then in our sports, wherein I have much delighted, and in that temptation, I confess, I did neglect and despise the offer, and lost that opportunity. Since that time God hath afflicted and chastised me, and my heart doth begin to break. And I have some great objections, which I cannot tell how to get over, which are still like great rocks in my way, over which I cannot climb. And if I should, I fear I shall fall down the precipice on the further side, and be spoiled and undone. By venturing to climb, I shall catch a deadly fall to me and my posterity.

The first objection that I have is this, because you praying Indians do reject your sachems, and refuse to pay them tribute, in so much that if any of my people turn to pray unto God, I do reckon that I have lost him. He will no longer own me for his sachem, nor pay me any tribute. And hence it will come to pass, that if I should pray to God, and all my people with me, I must become as a common man among them, and so lose all my power and authority over them. This is such a temptation as no other I, nor any of the great sachems, can tell how to get over. Were this temptation removed, the way would be more easy and open for me to turn praying Indian. I begin to have some good likance of the way, but I am loth to buy it at so dear a rate.[103]

It is a bit surprising that Eliot seems to have desired a frank representation of Metacomet's views, and though the above reflects a great deal of interpolation, it does show an honest and open side to Philip. Perhaps Eliot held out secret hope for his conversion, but the subsequent history reveals that Metacomet was unyielding in his resistance. According to Roger Williams, Eliot's Massachusett missionaries appar-

---

[103] Ibid., 121.

Hidden Genocide, Hidden People

ently issued threats of English retaliation if they did not adopt Christianity. In response, Williams sent off a letter to the General Court of Massachusetts Bay complaining of the practice:

> At my last departure for Engl. I was importun'd by the Nariganset Sachims and especially by Nenekunat, to present their peticion to the high Sachims of England that they might not be forced from their Religion, and for not changing their Religion be invaded by War. For they said they were dayly visited with Threatnings by Indians that came from about the Massachusets, that if they would not pray they should be destroyed by War.[104]

Williams passed along the above information directly to Oliver Cromwell in England, but military action had already been undertaken by the United Colonies with a force of mounted soldiers sent sweeping across Eastern Niantic territory. However, the force was unable to locate or define the 'enemy', and Massachusetts Bay promptly retreated from any other military actions against the Narragansetts and East Niantic allies, probably out of political concerns with their own relations with England. When the Narragansetts had voluntarily subjected themselves earlier to the English government, they had by law become full citizens with all the rights generally conferred by this status, and it would have created a political problem for Massachusetts Bay to attack them. More likely, the purpose was more akin to intimidation. But the issue here was not the Narragansetts' rights; indeed the real issue for the English government was the Puritans' stubborn tendency to ignore or bypass the authority of the English government in the first place. Nevertheless, Williams' intervention worked. It had become clear to Puritan religious and government leaders that the mission had stalled at the gates of the Narragansetts and the Wampanoags.

---

104 LaFantasie, ed., The Correspondence of Roger Williams, 409.

Chapter Six
The King Philip War and Genocide

It is observable that several of those nations which refused the gospel, quickly afterwards were so Devil driven as to begin an unjust and bloody war upon the English, which issued in their speedy and utter extirpation from the face of Gods earth. It was particularly remarked in Philip the ringleader of the most clamitous war that ever they made upon us; our Eliot made a tender of the everlasting Salvation to that king; but the monster entertained in with contempt and anger, and after the Native American mode of joining signs with words, he took a button upon the coat of the reverend man, adding, That he cared for his gospel just as much as he cared for that button. The world has heard what a terrrible ruine soon came upon that monarch, and upon all his people.[105]

Increase Mather

While Increase Mather, with a sense of absolute certainty and complete lack of shame, was able to put the blame for the King Philip War squarely on the Native Americans, most modern historians and students of American history take a more critical view, recognizing the clear bias in his report. Nevertheless, Mather's words have continued to reverberate and inform the debate even to the present day, clouding the clear fact of genocide and misconstruing the real cause of the war – Puritan aggression. Of course, many have looked to the more immediate causes of the war in order to determine which side was to blame, but that is a subterfuge. As a result, the debate over the long-term structural causes have been complicated by disagreements over the short term ones. Only three enduring facts remain undebated. First, there were many victims on all sides of the English and Native American conflict. Second, early documents focus mainly

---

[105] Increase Mather, The History of King Philip's War, Samuel G. Drake, ed. (Boston: Printed for the Editor, 1862), 208-209.

on the Puritan suffering during the war as a result of atrocities committed by the Native Americans. Third, the native voices are largely missing, though the few that were preserved in print carry a 'world of meaning'. While these above facts alone do not necessarily disparage nor contradict the authenticity of the narratives, it does suggest a need for critical analysis along with an active imagination.

Most historians in the past focused their attention upon the Wampanoag and Philip, but often ignored the Narragansetts. Puritan demands had been unremitting on this tribe. Nevertheless, the Narragansetts, with the help of English supporters, Roger Williams and others, had successfully staved off numerous military, economic, legal, cultural, and religious offensives without resorting to violence. All of this was a remarkable diplomatic achievement, considering the Puritan colonies virtually surrounded the proudly independent Narragansetts by the 1670's. Without the buffering effect of English settlers and the continued friendship of Roger Williams, even that history would have been undoubtedly meaner. It is a testimony to the integrity of Narragansett leaders that such a paradoxical situation could be resolved for as long as it was.

It is no secret that Rhode Island settlers, especially Roger Williams, admired the Narragansett sachems, Miantonomo and Canonicus, for their truthfulness, acumen, honor, and integrity. A history of peaceful, albeit strained, relations had passed, and neither the Narragansetts nor Puritans had given the other an opportunity or excuse for an outright attack. However, the increase of English settlers pouring into New England created pressure for land, and struggles for political and religious dominance threatened Narragansett autonomy. Narragansett leaders were fully aware of the precariousness of their situation and, more importantly, distrustful of Massachusetts Bay leaders. It is understandable that Canonicus would raise the subject of English intentions and trustworthiness with Williams in this narrative of a personal encounter between the two:

> Canounicus, the old high Sachim of the Nariganset Bay (a wise and peaceable Prince) once in a solemne Oration to my self, in a solemne assembly, using this word, said, I have never suffered any wrong to be be offered to the English since they landed; nor never

will: he often repeated this word, Wunnaumwayean, Englishman; if the englishman speake true, if hee meane truly, then shall I goe to my grave in peace, and hope that the English and my posterite shall live in love and peace together. I replied, that he had no cause (as I hoped) to question Englishmans, Wunnaumwauonck, that is, faithfulnesse, he having had long experience of their friendlinesse and trustinesse. He tooke a sticke and broke it into ten pieces, and related ten instances (laying downe a sticke to every instance) which gave him cause thus to feare and say; I satisfied him in some presently, and presented the rest to the Governours of the english, who, I hope, will be far from giving just cause to have Barbarians to question their Wunnaumwauonck, or faithfulness.[106]

Canounicus' suspicions were well founded. Puritan agents had attempted numerous times to encroach on Narragansett territory, but none of the efforts had fully succeeded. The Narragansetts had ruled their affairs well, and for years there was no Puritan colony that would dare risk the wrath of Parliament by conducting a war of conquest against them without a good excuse. But that did not stop other forms of encroachment and treachery conducted at the topmost layers of Puritan government.

In 1660, a Royal Commission was sent to New England to investigate charges that the colonies had transacted a fraudulent contract with the Narragansetts under the sponsorship of John Winthrop, Jr.. But a more important role of the Commission included the authority to seize the territory of New York under its direct control. Through that seizure, it also claimed jurisdiction over Rhode Island and a large portion of Connecticut west of the Connecticut River. With the Commission's extension of New York authority into Rhode Island, Connecticut was surrounded on two sides by Royalist colonies. The action of the Commission also redefined the border areas of Rhode Island to include the territory upon which the main body of the Wampanoags lived, Mount Hope (Bristol, RI). That, in turn, threatened Plimoth, which

---

[106] Williams, *A Key Into the Language of America*, 57-58.

relied heavily upon the Wampanoag presence as a hedge against other English encroachers in their territory. As a result of all these maneuverings, both the Wampanoags and Narragansetts were further weakened and isolated from each other.

Mount Hope, the home of King Philip and the Pokanoket Wampanoags, sat on the Peninsula jutting out on the eastern portion of Narragansett Bay in the vicinity of present-day Bristol, Rhode Island. Various tributary tribes, also known as Wampanoags extended throughout southeastern Massachusetts, including Cape Cod, Martha's Vineyard and Nantucket. But Plimoth encroachment had gradually squeezed the Wampanoags into smaller and more isolated regions. Nevertheless, under Massasoit's leadership, most of the Wampanoags had remained faithful to their pledges to the English throughout the years, and peace had been maintained. In part, this was due to the treaty signed by Massasoit and the Pilgrims, under which the Wampanoags faced a different legal situation than Native Americans elsewhere in New England. Under the terms of their contract with the Wampanoags, and by the standards of English law, the Plimoth colony was ironically sanctioned through its role as a Protectorate of the Wampanoags.

Although the Wampanoags had been alternately pressured by Plimoth, they had been able to maintain their independence and neutrality through diplomatic means. The long period of peaceful coexistence had been partly due to the influence of Massasoit. Massasoit had been able to maintain the independence of his tribe in the face of shrinking territory, along with various abuses and insults perpetrated by their English neighbors. Out of all the major tribes of southern New England, only the Wampanoags had been successful in resisting coercion and pressure to subject itself to the English, but it had done so through an unequal client relationship with its legal patron in Plimoth. This changed once Plimoth received full recognition by the English government, and the presence of the Wampanoags became superfluous.

Eventually Plimoth would come to dominate and bully the Wampanoags, despite the forbearance of Massasoit and other sachems of the tribe toward the English. The bullying increased upon Massasoit's death and the ascendance of his son, Wamsutta, to the position of sachem at Mount Hope. Wamsutta was an independent-minded sachem, like his father. When Massasoit asserted his own independence by selling

The King Phillip War and Genocide

Roger Williams a parcel of land near Providence without first seeking permission, the Plimoth government overlooked it. But Plimoth was not about to let Wamsutta get away with any such thing. When rumors and accusations flew in Plimoth concerning Wamsutta's intention to sell more land to non-Plimoth residents, Plimoth responded by sending a small military detachment to demand that Wamsutta accompany them to Plimoth to answer for the rumors. Under pressure, he relented and agreed to accompany them.

Wamsutta never arrived in Plimoth. He suddenly became sick during the journey, and the military detachment freed him to return home. Wamsutta never returned home either, dying from his mysterious illness on the way back. The Plimoth leaders promptly washed their hands of the affair, and rumors that Wamsutta had actually been poisoned broke out. Of course, there is no way to prove or disprove the rumors. Nevertheless, the whole incident had given the Wampanoags a reason to resist and rebel. Life under Plimoth had become hazardous to their health. This was the obvious lesson taken when Metacomet [King Philip] inherited his dead brother's position as sachem at Mount Hope during June, 1664.

Plimoth lost no time trying to dictate terms to Wamsutta's brother, Metacomet (King Philip), was immediately pressured under threats to sign a new treaty outlawing any Wampanoag land sales to non-Plimoth settlers. The Wampanoags didn't have any choice in the matter, and he signed. But the action demonstrated that the Plimoth Colony had altered its policy and attitude toward the Wampanoags. In 1667, Plimoth encroached even further into Wampanoag territory, violating earlier treaties and established the town of Swansea ten miles from Mount Hope. But even as Plimoth sought to expand its domain, as a result of a decision of the Royal Commission in England, boundaries between Massachusetts Bay, Plimoth, Rhode Island, and Connecticut were all thrown into dispute.

In New England, realization was growing among many Native Americans, especially the Wampanoag, that traditional means of coping through non-violent resistance had failed to stem the tide of English conquest, exploitation and corruption. As a result, a more belligerent mood broke out, and manifested in several ways. Most important, by the 1660's, Native Americans were able to procure guns and other armaments through a variety of channels, including Dutch, English and French. As a result, English mistrust and fear escalated rapidly, especially when groups such as Metacomet's began to show resistance to English offenses in speech and gestures, particularly in displays of armed force.

Despite Plimoth's domination of the neighboring Wampanoags, it was the most vulnerable of all the colonies, mainly from the military and legal encroachments of Massachusetts Bay, but also the many Royalist forces surrounding them in the region. Plimoth was also threatened by the Royal Commission's proposed realignment of boundaries, mainly because it would place the Wampanoags at Mount Hope under the jurisdiction of Rhode Island. Plimoth's reaction was to step up its persecution of the tribe, determined that it alone should have proprietary rights over them. Plimoth even tried to circumvent the Commision's decision by pressuring Metacomet to subject his tribe directly to Plimoth authority. When Metacomet refused, Plimoth leaders were reportedly furious at him. This, of course would have been inconsistent with English law, not to mention Wampanoag custom. On the other hand, Plimoth had thus far bullied them into virtual submission on a whole range of issues, if only to demonstrate their ultimate authority. Nevertheless, one can readily understand Metacomet's refusal to give in on this issue. Drake writes concerning his reasoning on this point:

> It is said that shortly before the War of 1675 began, the Governor of Massachusetts sent to inquire of Philip why he would war upon the English, and to request him to enter into a Treaty. The Sachem replied: "Your Governor is but a Subject of King Charles of England; I shall not treat with a Subject, I shall treat of Peace only with the King my Brother. When he comes I am ready.[107]

From the beginning of his ascendancy to the position of Sachem, Plimoth had continued to call Metacomet's intentions into question, repeatedly accusing him of defiance of their orders, and demanding him to give up many Wampanoag rights. More importantly, he was

---

[107]Samuel G. Drake. Biography and History of the Indians of North America. (Boston: Benjamin B. Mussey, & Co., 1841).

required to disarm his people, an action which he did not have the authority to command by Algonquin custom. Of course, this was understood by English colonists, but Plimoth threatened him if he did not sign a statement to that effect. Following is a copy of the text, notably filled with accusations, inaccuracies and unfounded assertions, which Plimoth authorities required of Metacomet and his people:

> Whereas my Father, my Brother, and my self, have formally submitted ourselves and our People unto the Kings Majesty of England, and to the Colony of New Plimoth, by solemn Covenant under our Hand; but I having of late through my Indiscretion, and the Naughtiness of my Heart, violated and broken this my Covenant with my Friends, by taking up Arms, with evil intent against them, and that groundlessly; I being now deeply sensible of my Unfaithfulness and Folly, do desire at this Time solemnly to renew my Covenant with my ancient Friends, and my Father's Friends above mentioned, and do desire that this may testifie to the World against me if ever I shall again fail in my Faithfulness towards them (that I have now, and at all Times found so kind to me) or any other of the English Colonies; and as a real Pledg of my true Intentions for the Future to be Faithful and Friendly, I do freely engage to resign up unto the Government of New Plimouth, all my English Arms, to be kept by them for their Security, so long as they shall see Reason. For true Performance of the Premises, I have hereunto set my Hand, together with the Rest of my Council.[108]

Of course, the above treaty exacerbated the already deteriorating relations between Plimoth and Wampanoags, and it continued to reverberate and further exacerbate tensions. Metacomet himself was reported to have misunderstood it, believing that it pertained to the group

---

[108] Samuel G. Drake, ed., The History of the Indian Wars in New England (Roxbury, MA: W. Elliot Woodward, 1865), vol. 1, "A Narrative of the Troubles With The Indians (1677)", by William Hubbard, 54-55.

Hidden Genocide, Hidden People

of armed warriors who had accompanied him to the meeting, and not the entire Wampanoag confederacy. It is clear that Plimoth wanted the total subjection and disarmament of the Wampanoags under their control, while the Wampanoags refused to turn in their weapons.

As tensions grew between Plimoth and the Wampanoag, rumors spread that the Narragansetts intended to participate in a combined Native American conspiracy to war against the English, putting Metacomet at the center of it. While these rumors were unsubstantiated, they were propagated by clerical authorities such as William Hubbard, the foremost Puritan historian of the King Philip War:

> Yet did this treacherous and perfidious Caitiff still harbor the same or more mischievous Thoughts against the English than ever before, and hath been since that Time plotting with all the Native Americans round about to make a general Insurrection against the English in all the Colonies; which, as some Prisoners lately brought in have confessed, should have been put in Execution at once, by all the Native Americans rising as one Man, against all those Plantations of English which were next them." he wrote, ironically accusing the Native Americans of a conspiracy.[109]

Hubbard was not satisfied only with maligning Metacomet, and further maligned Native Americans in general:

> That the Indians had a Conspiracy amongst themselves to rise against the English, is confirmed by some of the Native Americans, about Hadly [Waban, early in 1675, reported to Gen. Gookin, that he had reason to believe the Indians intended to begin War as soon as the Trees were leaved out.], although the plot was not come to Maturity when Philip began, the special Providence of God therein over-ruling the Contrivers: For when the Beginning of the Troubles first was reported from Mount Hope, many of the Indians were in a kind of Maze, not knowing well what to do;

---

[109] Ibid., 58

The King Phillip War and Genocide

> sometimes ready to stand for the English, as formerly they were wont to do, sometimes inclining to strike in with Philip (which at the last they generally did) which if it had been foreseen, much of that mischief might have been prevented that fell out in several Places, more by perfidious and treacherous Dealing than any other Ways: the English never imagining that after so many obliging Kindnesses received from them by the Indians, besides their many Engagements and protestations of Friendship, as formerly, they would have been so Ungrateful, perfidiously False and Cruel as they have since proved.[110]

While Hubbard's words attempted to demonstrate the strategic necessity for the war, a religious rationale for genocide was also needed in order to build public support for it. Rev. Increase Mather, one of the most influential leaders of his day, repeatedly insisted that the rejection of the gospel had been the cause of the King Philip War. As a public figure, he was especially unremitting and venomous in his attacks upon Native Americans, casting his rhetoric in the same typological style as his predecessors, particularly John Cotton and John Wilson. Born in Boston and steeped in the Puritan worldview, Mather created a stereotype of Native Americans as hopelessly evil, and predestined to play out a critical role in the cosmic battleground of New England; for Mather, that ultimately meant genocide at the hands of the Puritans. It could not be made any simpler. In 1674, at the prelude of the King Philip War, Mather's words must have thundered forth from the pulpit like those of his predecessor, remnants of which are preserved in his writings. Thus, in preparing the people for war and releasing the bloodlust that would lead to genocide, he proclaimed:

> There is a black Cloud over our heads, which begins to drop upon us. Providence hath so ordered, that our Enemies are come near, and may we not then think tht trouble is near? The Lord hath been whetting his glittering Sword a long time; we have heard a noise, and a dismall din hath been in our ears, but

---

[110] ibid., 59-60.

> now the Sword seems to be facing and marching directly towards us: yet we see Jerusalem compassed about with Enemies. Christ said unto his Disciples, Luke 21:20. When ye shall see Jerusalem compassed with Enemies, then know that the desolation thereof is nigh. Is not our Jerusalem compassed with armies? There are pretended Friends at our backs, and professed Enemies before our faces. The sky looketh red and lowring, we may therefore fear, that foul Weather is at hand: As once that Prophet said, There is a found an abundance of Rain, and in the mean-while, the Heaven was black with Clouds. Truly so it is at this day, the Heavens are black over our heads. The Clouds begin to gather thick in our Horizon: yea, there is a Cloud of Blood, which begins to drop upon us. When once a Cloud begins to drop, you know that a Shower is wont to follow. The Cloud of Blood over our heads begins to drop; there was one drop fell the other day, witness the man that was slain upon the Coasts: the Lord grant that a Shower of Blood may not follow. [111]

Mather's opinion of Native Americans was diametrically opposed to Eliot's exalted vision of the Native Americans as the precursers of the millenium. For Mather, the Native Americans appeared to have no intrinsic value as human beings, except insofar as they played a role in the purification of the Puritan Commonwealth. Mather consistently ascribed wicked and demonic intentions to Native Americans, revealing both a cosmic portent and a clear rationale for waging a preemptive and genocidal war. Ironically, the foil for this unfolding cosmic battle was the death of Eliot's understudy, Massachusett missionary, John Sausaman (aka. Wassausmon and Sassamon).

> No doubt but one reason why the Indians murdered John Sausaman was out of hatred against him for his Religion, for he was Christianized and baptiz'd,

---

[111] Increase Mather, "The Day of Trouble is Near ", in <u>Increase Mather: Jeremiads</u>, Sacvan Bercovitch, ed. (New York: AMS Press Inc. ,1984), 26.

and was a Preacher amongst the Native Americans, being of very excellent parts, he translated some part of the Bible into the Indian language, and was wont to curb those Indians that knew not God, on the account of their debaucheries; but the main ground why they murthered him seems to be, because he discovered their subtle and malicious designs, which they were complotting against the English.[112]

The facts in the above case demonstrate the duplicity of Mather's words. Sausaman had been found dead in a pond near Marshfield, Massachusetts. Three Wampanoag men were then accused of the death and executed by hanging, but that was not all. Under torture, one of them confessed that Metacomet had ordered Sausaman's murder. This would suggest a strange and inconsistent motive for Metacomet, and there is no evidence to support Mather's contention that it was intended as a direct assault upon Eliot's mission. It was a convenient ploy, however. By late winter in 1675, Plimoth forces had already been deployed within ten miles of Metacomet's village.

There are much better sources for Metacomet's thoughts on the causes of the war only weeks before its start. In this atmosphere of threats, distrust and tension, the Lieutenant Governor of Rhode Island, a down-to-earth practical minded Quaker named John Easton, led a small delegation of Rhode Islanders to visit Metacomet at Mount Hope (Bristol, RI). This optimistic Quaker went hoping to mediate a non-violent outcome to the growing conflict. His written account of the meeting with Metacomet is extremely noteworthy, perhaps the most objective and revealing source document concerning the causes of the war. The transcript shows that both Metacomet and Easton made an attempt to honestly hear and record the concerns and issues expressed by each other at the meeting. Below is Easton's rather lengthy but instructive narrative relating, in a colloquial local dialect, his meeting with Metacomet on the eve of the war:

> About four Miles we had to cum; thither our Messenger cum tothem; they not aware of it behaved themselves as furious, but suddenly apealed when

---

[112] Mather, The History King Philip's War, 48.

they understood who he was and what he came for, he called his Counsell and agreed to cum to us; came himself unarmed, and about 40 of his Men armed. Then 5 of us went over, 3 wear Mgistrates. We sate veri friendly together. We told him our bisnes was to indever that they might not refeue or do Rong. They said that was well; they had dun no Rong, the English ronged them. We said we knew the English said the Indians ronged them, and the Indians said the English ronged them, but our Desier was the Quarrell might rightly be decided, in the best Way, and not as Dogs desided theier Quarrells. The Native Americans owned yt fighting was the worst Way; then they propounded how Right might take Place. We said, by Arbitration. They said that all English agreed against them, and so by Arbitration they had had much Rong; mani Miles square of Land so taken from them, for English wold have English Arbitrators; and once they were persuaded to give in their Armes, yt thereby Jealousy might be removed, and the English having theier Arms wold not deliver them as they had promised, until they consented to pay a 100L , and now they had not so much Sum or Muny; yt thay wear as good be kiled as leave all ther Liveflyhode.

We said they might chuse a Indian King and the English might chuse the Governor of New Yorke, yt nether had Case to say either wear Parties in the Diferance. They said they had not heard of yt way, and said we onestly spoke, so we wear perswaided if yt Way had bine tendered they would have acsepted. We did endeaver not to hear theier Complaints, said it was not convenient for us now to consider of, but to indever to prevent War; said to them when in War against English, Blood was spilt, yt ingaged all Englishmen, for we wear to be all under one King; we knew what their Complains wold be, and in our Colony had removed some of them in sending fo

The King Phillip War and Genocide

Native American Rulers in what the Crime concerned Native Americans Lives, which thay veri lovingly acsepted, and agreed with us to their Execution, and said so they were abell to satisfie their Subjects when they knew an Native American sufered duly, but said in what was only between their Native Americans and not in Towneshipes, yt we had purchased, they wold not have us prosecute, and yt that thay had a great Fear to have ani of ther Indian should be caled or forced to be Christian Indians. Thay said yt such wer in everi thing more mischievous, only Disemblers, and then the English made them not subject to ther Kings, and by thier lying to rong ther Kings. We knew it to be true, and we promising them yt however in Government to Native Americans all should be alike, and yt we knew it ws our King's will it should be so, yt altho we wear weaker than other Colonies, they having submitted to our King to protect them, others dare not otherwise to molest them; expressed thay took that to be well, that we had littell Case to doute, but that to us under the King thay would hav yielded to our Determinations in what ani shold have complained to us against them.

But Philip charged it to be disonestly in us to be put of the Hering to just Complaints, therefore we consented to hear them. Thay said they had bine the first in doing Good to the English, and the English the first in doing Rong; said when the English first came, their IKing's Father was as a great Man, and the English as a littell Child; he constrained other Native Americans from ronging the English, and gave them Corn and shewed them how to plant, and was free to do them ani Good, and had let them have a 100 times more Land than now the King had for his own Peopell. But ther King's Brother, when he ws King, came miserably to dy by being forced to Court, as they judge poysoned. And another Greavance was, if 20 of there onest Native Americans testified that a Englisman had dun them Rong, it ws as nothing; and if but one of the worst Native Americans testified against any Indian or ther King, when it pleased the English it was sufitiant. Another Grievance was, when their King sold Land, the English wold say, it ws more than they agreed to, and a Writing must be prove against all them, and sum o their Kings had dun Rong to sell so much. He left his Peopell none, and sum being given to Drunknes the English made them drunk and then cheated them in Bargains, but now ther Kings ear forewarned not for to part with Land, for nothing in Cumparison to the Value thereof. Now home the English had owned for King of Queen, they wold disinheret, and make another King that wold give or fell them these Lands; that now, they had no Hopes left to kepe ani Land. Another Grievance, the English Catell and Horses still incresed; that when thay removed 30 Mill from where English had ani thing to do, they could not kepe ther Corn from being spoyled, they never being used to fence, and thost when the English bost Land of them thay wold have kept their Catell upon ther owne Land. Another Grievance, the English were so eager to sell the Native Americans Lickers, yt most of the Native Americans spent all in Drynknes, and then rauved upon the sober Native Americans, and thay did believe often did hurt the English Catell, and ther King could not prevent it.

So we departed without ani Discurtiousness, and sudingly had Letter from Plimoth Governor thay intended in Arms to conforem Philip, but no Information what yt was thay required or wt Termes he refused to have their Quarrell desided; and in a Weke's Time after we had bine with the Indians the War thus

---

[113] ibid.,15-16.

begun.[113]

At the start of the war, things did not seem to go so well for the Puritan and Plimoth forces, despite an overwhelming advantage in weaponry. Their initial strategy had been to isolate Metacomet's people at Mount Hope, but the tactic failed, probably the most crucial mistake of the campaign for the English, for it allowed the united Wampanoags to instead fight the war in English territory. The Wampanoags knew how to live off the land as well as travel quickly through it, giving them a distinct advantage by providing the element of surprise attacks on the widely scattered and relatively remote English towns. By comparison, the English were clumsy, preferring to stick to the open fields, particularly in battle. Thus the English were further disadvantaged in this war by the nature of the terrain and their inability to move with neither speed nor secrecy.

The first few months were brutal ones for the Puritans. Once the Plimoth armies allowed Metacomet and his Mount Hope Wampanoags to escape, various other Wampanoag communities were drawn into the conflict. As it progressed, the war became increasingly racial, with both sides perceiving it to be a final showdown between the English and Native Americans in the region, which was accurate. It should also be mentioned that among Metacomet's forces was a large group of Wampanoags under the sachem, Weetamoo, often referred to in Puritan writings as the "squaw sachem". Weetamoo figured prominently in the course of the war, despite evidence that she had been drawn rather unwillingly into the battle.

While it would be impractical here to recite fully the events of the war, it is important to make some characterizations. Late summer of 1675 found the English colonies in shock over their losses. While Puritan forces had exacted large tolls against Native American non-combatants, the forces under Metacomet's leadership had continued to wreak havoc against English towns. This was a war of unabated violence, with tortures and massacres of combatants and non-combatants perpetrated by English and Native American alike. Once engaged, the proverbial 'lid blew off the kettle', and desperation and fear appear to have stricken the Puritan colonists, resulting in the abandonment of a large number of inland communities, and seriously affecting the food supply of the new colonies. At first, Connecticut remained secure from attacks, although it too had committed forces, especially along the upper reaches of the Connecticut River near the vulnerable river towns of Springfield, Pawcumtuck, Hadley, and others. And indeed, the spring of 1676 brought the war to this region with a vengeance. But in the summer of 1675, much of the violence centered upon the outlying towns of Massachusetts Bay and Plimoth colonies.

The war promoted a radical shift in Puritan theology from one based in typology to one with a more apocalyptic orientation. Clergy described the Puritans as an "army of Christ" engaged in a great battle between the forces of good and evil. As the war progressed, however, mounting losses posed a dilemma for theologians and clergy, failing to find an adequate explanation for the rapidly multiplying English deaths. The sign seekers, the clergy in this instance, took the helm and put their prodigious pens to the tasks, but much of the writing took on a visceral note. Native American deaths, of course, were seen as a vindication of the righteousness of the Puritan cause. But how to account for failures has always been a crucial stumbling block in any religiously motivated war, and this one was no different; one must find a religious explanation in order to justify war. So, in response to a very gloomy and desperate circumstances, the clergy blamed and decried their own people for their sins, proclaiming that their god was punishing them with bodily losses and sufferings for their disobedience. One can only imagine the effects on the common people, accused of causing the deaths of their brethren by a lack of religious zeal and righteous behavior. At the very least, the reaction must have been one of fear and confusion, at least, albeit a good reason to cringe on a cold church bench without food in the belly. A public appeal was sent out to all towns, announcing that their god was calling for an act of public humiliation through acts of prayer, fasting and contrition. The following text is an example. It was written by Increase Mather, printed as a broadside and posted throughout the colony:

> Octob. the 7th. This day of Humiliation appointed by the Council, was solemnly observed: Yet attended with awfull testimonyes of divine displeasure. The very next day after the Fast was agreed upon by those in civill Authority, was that dismal and fatal blow, when Captain Lothrop and his company (in all near

The King Phillip War and Genocide

upon four score souls) were slaughtered, whereby the Heathen were wonderfully animated, some of them triumphing and saying, that so great slaughter was never known: and indeed in the Warrs one with another, the like hath rarely been heard of. And that very day when this Fast was kept, three Persons were killed by the Indians near Dover, one of them going from the publick Worship. ..." continues- "And inasmuch as this conclusion this news came at the conclusion of a day of Humiliation, surely the solemn voice of God to New England is still as formerly, Praying without Reforming will not do. And now is the day come wherein the Lord is fulfilling the word which himself hath spoken, saying, I will send wild Beast among you, which shall rob you of your Children, and destroy your Cattle... .[114]

In representing the conflict in such stark and apocalyptical terms, Mather was actually representing a new twist on the old typological themes of Puritanism. The new theme was the idea of a broken covenant; thus it was the failure of the community to faithfully execute the terms of the covenant which had caused disaster. Another aspect of Mather's analysis draws attention to itself, namely his assertion that the Native Americans, "in their Warrs one with another, the like hath rarely been heard of." Indeed, the King Philip War was a different type of war for the Native Americans of New England. Mather's interpretation here is consistent with many other observers of Algonquin culture. Massive warfare, massacres, tortures, and violence against non-combatants violated Algonquin custom, and was repulsive to them. The Wampanoag did not suffer from 'blood lust', but rather were motivated by desperation. By attributing the Lathropp massacre to divine displeasure as opposed to Wampanoag desperation, Mather was stretching the limits of typology beyond previous understandings. Its influence was immediate. The Puritan colonies became determined to reverse the course of the war and, in the bargain, purge their territories once and for all of all manifestations of evil, namely Native Americans. This included the Wampanoags, and the list soon grew to include the Nip-

---

[114] Mather, The History of the King Philip's War, 95.

mucs, Connecticut River tribes, Narragansetts, and others, all in the name of Christ, many of them praying towne Native Americans or "Eliot's Native Americans", a term used by many residents throughout the colony.

As the war proceeded, Puritans lashed out against Quakers and other non-conformers in their midst. Many Quakers were persecuted, and some were made to run the "gauntlet" as a brutal physical punishment for not joining the fight against the Native Americans; it is estimated that approximately fifty percent of those forced through this brutal treatment died as a result. As the war continued into the winter, mob action became rampant throughout the colonies as furious colonists took out their resentment on the residents of neighboring "praying townes". The harassment had a legal component, as laws were enacted disarming all Native Americans in Puritan territories, making them easy prey for criminals. Other laws were even more odious, restricting Native Americans to their townes, and giving legal rights to English colonists to kill any Native American travelling outside of their villages. The restrictions fell upon Massachusetts, Nipmucs and Penacooks alike, including those who lived outside the range of Puritan territory. Dominion had finally led to tyranny, and by early winter that led to policy-driven genocide.

Perhaps the most revealing of Puritan military operations at the beginning of the war can be found in the decision to preemptively attack the neutral Narragansetts. In the end, the Narragansetts did not comply with Puritan demands because they, having subjected themselves to the King in 1643, concluded that they were equal to any other political entity in New England – with every legal justification it might include. Under the circumstances it was probably the most viable option for the Narragansetts, but they obviously didn't realize just how brazen the Puritan enterprise had become.

Despite the intention of the Narragansetts to remain neutral in the King Philip War, Massachusetts Bay was evidently convinced that they could turn the situation to their own advantage. Since neither Massachusetts Bay, Connecticut nor Plimoth were willing to accept the autonomy of the Narragansetts nor any other Native American tribe in New England, Massachusetts Bay decided to take the offensive by calling together the infamous "Star Chamber", a meeting of the Com-

The King Phillip War and Genocide

missioners of the United Colonies on November 2, 1675. The Commissioners, sweeping aside all legal and moral objections, and without evidence of Narragansett complicity in the war, decided to invade without just and sufficient cause. It was a purely pragmatic decision, driven by Puritan fears. The ante was being raised. William Hubbard describes the Commissioners' decision and rationale for an unprovoked offensive engagement against the Narragansetts' major village – conducting a massacre in the middle of winter:

> On the other Hand it was considered, that if the Enemy were let alone till the next Summer, it would be impossible to deal with them, or find them any where, but they might waste one Company of Soldiers after another, as was seen by the Experience of the former Year. Considering also that the Narhagansets, the most Numerous of all the Rest, and best provided of Provision of all the other Indians, had now declared themselves our Enemies, who if they were let alone till the Winter was over, we should be unable to deal with so many Enemies at once, that could on a sudden, on any occasion, spread themselves like Grashoppers all over the Country. It was therefore agreed upon by the general consent of all, to fall upon the winter-quarters of our Enemies, by a more considerable Army (if I may so call it) gathered out of all the three Colonies, and that with all Expedition, as furthest not exceed the tenth of December, before they should have a thousand Men in Arms ready for the Design.[115]

Thus, in practical consideration of an imaginary threat, the Commissioners decided upon a course that would destroy the Narragansetts in a single stroke. The genocidal action began on December 19, 1675, when the above plan was put into motion with a combined force of over one thousand soldiers, with a purpose to kill and destroy the Narragansetts, most of whom were in their winter quarters, a fortified town in the midst of a swamp. Alongside a core of experienced sol-

---

[115] **Hubbard, The History of the Indian Wars in New England, 134-135.**

Hidden Genocide, Hidden People

diers, many volunteers were recruited with the lure of war booty, having been promised a piece of Narragansett land following the military action. This well-armed force was able to pull off a surprise attack due to a renegade Narragansett-turned traitor who led them secretly to the town. In addition, an early freeze made it possible for the main body of troops to cross en masse toward the objective, rather than in single files, in the vent of the terrain been wet and unfrozen. All together, it worked to the Puritan's advantage by allowing the army to encircle the fortification before being discovered. Once the element of surprise was broached, a furious fight ensued for the first hour or so until the English troops were able to force their way past the barricades surrounding the fort. English troops then torched the hundreds of wigwams in which many of the frightened women, children, and elders had hidden while the warriors were busy fighting the soldiers outside. A huge maelstrom of flames engulfed the village making escape impossible. Just as in the massacre of the Pequots at Mystic in 1637, the English surrounded the burning dwellings and killed those who attempted to flee. Following is William Hubbard's very sardonic description of the dreadful scene:

> It is reported by them that first entered the Indians Fort, that our Soldiers came upon them when they were ready to dress their Dinner; but one sudden and unexpected Assault put them besides that Work, making their Cookrooms too hot for them at that Time, when they and their Mitchin fryed together.[116]

While the Narragansett massacre undoubtedly became a source of boasting for Hubbard and undoubtedly many colonists, it achieved little in the way of strategic advantage, and perhaps the opposite. The attack had killed mainly women and children. Most of the Narragansett warriors were engaged in battle and hadn't been able to save them. Once the wigwams went up in flames, the surviving warriors were forced to retreat into the welcoming winter camps of the Wampanoags and Nipmucs in central Massachusetts. So, instead of weakening the enemy, the surprise attack compounded problems for the Puritans; now there were Narragansetts along with several thousand others poised on the western borders, ready for spring when movement would be pos-

---

[116] Ibid., 148.

sible and attacks conducted. This recognition must have shaken the Puritan leaders, who were bombarded by apocalyptic visions of Puritan preachers, warning of woes to come.

Following the attack on the Narragansetts, Massachusetts Bay began a new wave of oppression, this time aiming their wrath and suspicions at Native Americans in the praying towns. In a fit of histrionics and despite John Eliot and Daniel Gookin's protests, the authorities in Mass Bay ordered Native Americans living in "praying townes" (such as Natick) imprisoned for the winter at Deer Island and on other isolated islands along the coast. It was a horrific policy resulting in slow torture associated with freezing and starvation. As is well documented, the vast majority died during that imprisonment. The order has been remembered as one of the most inhumane and irrational decisions made during the King Philip War, although there were many others as well.

The brutal policies of the Puritans were further compounded by the composition of military personnel, many of whom were economically dependent upon a successful outcome. Many men in the Puritan forces had been conscripted or lured into the campaign with promises of booty and land grants upon the success of conquest. Others were paid mercenaries, many with sordid backgrounds as pirates and criminals. One of these men was Captain Samuel Mosely, a former pirate who was put in charge of a company composed largely of pirates and various criminals who received acquittals in return for their military service. Mosely was a controversial figure, even amongst the colonists for his violent and brutal treatment of Native Americans. Robert Kent Diebold provides a succinct and vivid description of the brutal company of soldiers led by Mosely:

> A swaggering braggert, Mosely was by far the most colorful and popular officer in the English army. Frequently insolent to his superiors, he was protected by his popularity and by his marriage to the niece of the Massachusetts governor. During the war, his company seems to have travelled with a pack of dogs, used to terrorize Native Americans. In October, he was to capture an Native American woman near Hatfield; after she provided him with information, he had her "torn to peeces by Doggs," a fact about which he boasts in a

letter to the Massachusetts Council.[117]

The cruelty of Moseley and other mercenaries during the King Philip War is legendary. Perhaps the most tragic aspect of this cruelty was its impact upon those Native Americans who lived in the "praying townes". Many of the most gruesome atrocities of the war were inflicted upon these non-combatants, which infuriated even some of the staunchest Puritans, notably John Eliot and Daniel Gookin. The atrocities undermined the Puritan missions and made it impossible to rebuild the trust with those Native Americans who were brutally punished. Eliot must have been flabbergasted at the wholesale persecution of those who had persevered in order to gain their salvation. Nathaniel Saltonstall narrates an important incident revealing the scope of the persecution at the end of the war, and Eliot and Gookin's efforts to block it:

> Towards the latter End of August, Captain Moseley took eight Indians alive, and sent them Prisoners to Boston, who were put in Prison there; these were of the Number of Mr. Elliot's Indians; (as also many of those Native Americans that were shipt off by Captain Sprague, for the Straits and Cales). These Men were at several times tried for their Lives, and condemned to die: Mean Time Mr. Elliot and Captain Guggins pleded so very hard for the Indians, that the whole Council knew not what to do about them. They hearkened to Mr. Elliot for his Gravity, Age, and Wisdom, and also for that he hath been the chief Instrument that the Lord hath made use of, in Propagating the Gospel among the Heathen; And was their teacher, till the time that some Indians were brought up in the University to supply his place.[118]

But Eliot and Guggins' words were not enough to win the release of the innocent captives. Eliot and Gookin were up against an intransigent Council and irate public willing to exact punishment on any and all Native Americans, regardless of guilt or innocence. That night, before injustice could be administered, some sympathetic souls (Eliot

---

[117] Robert Ken Diebold, "A Critical Edition of Mrs. Mary Rowlandson's Captivity Narrative", (Ph.D. diss., Yale University, 1962) xiv.

The King Phillip War and Genocide

and Gookin) were able to sneak in to where the Native Americans were imprisoned and set most of them free. The next day a lynch mob gathered, infuriated by Eliot and Gookin, and demanded the Justice of the Peace to issue an immediate order of execution against the one captive caught in flight. Here is the description of the horrific episode, again told in Saltonstall's words:

> For the Commonality were so enraged against Mr. Elliot and Captain Guggins (Gookin) especially, that Captain Guggins said on the Bench, that he was afraid to go along the Streets; the Answer was made, you may thank yourself; however and Order was issued out for the Execution of that one (notorious above the rest) Native American, and accordingly he was led by a Rope about his Neck to the Gallows; when he came there, the Executioners (for there were many) flung one End over the Poset, and so hoised him up like a Dog, three or four Times, he being yet half alive and half dead; then came an Native American, a Friend of his, and with his Knife made a Hole in his Breast to his Heart, and sucked out his Heart-Blood: Being asked his Reason therefore, his Answer, Umh, Umh nu, Me stronger as I was before, me be so strong as me and he too, he be ver strong Man fore he die.[119]

During the winter of 1675 many Wampanoags and others withdrew to the area around Mount Wachusett, but Metacomet led a large group further west to an area just north of Albany to spend the winter in safety from Puritan forces. Unfortunately, it was perhaps the biggest blunder of the war for Metacomet's forces. The Mohawks' surprise attack killed several hundred of Metacomet's best warriors. This was the direct result of Gov. Edmund Andros of New York who, in a calculated move to influence the outcome of the war in New York's favor, instigated the attack by the Mohawks. Andros had earlier tried to intervene in the war, and had even sent a well armed ship to Connecticut with orders for the colony to recognize the King's authority through the now

---

[118] Nathaniel Saltonstall, "The Present State of New England With Respect to the Indian War ", in <u>Narratives of the Indian Wars</u>, Charles H. Lincoln, ed. (New York: Barnes and Noble, Inc., 1959), 40.

Hidden Genocide, Hidden People

dominant New York government. But Connecticut refused to stand down, and sent Andros' ship back with the reply that his help was not needed or appreciated in New England. Andros resorted then to the tactic of spreading false rumors of a general insurrection against the Puritans. Andros wrote the following in a letter to the Deputy Governor of Connecticut during the Autumn of 1675:

> An Indyan under a Pretence of friendship, telling and affirming very confidently, to one of this place, That there is an extraordinary Confederacy between all the neighboring Indyans and eastwards, (in wch yor pretended friends to bee included) and designed this light Moone, to attack Hartford itselfe, and some other Places about Greenwch, of which being informed this Morning, I have immediately despatches this, to give you Accot thereof, lest there should bee some Thing in it, though not so much as they report, 5 or 6000 Indyans enjoyned together.[120]

The uneven and volatile relations between Andros and the Puritan colonies must have been an omen to those in New England fearful of royalist intervention. By the spring of 1676, as a result of Andros' unsolicited incitement of Mohawk forces against Metacomet's people during the previous winter, the war with the Native Americans had shifted determinedly in favor of the Puritan forces. The rebel forces were desperately weakened by the combination of the swamp massacre in Rhode Island and the battle losses in New York. A winter of famine, illness, and other privations in their winter campsites around Mt. Wachusett had also wreaked havoc on the spirits and strength of the combined tribes. Southern New England must have seemed a lost cause for those left uprooted from their homeland. Even if Metacomet and allies were able to drive out the Puritans, the royalist governor of New York and the might of the English empire were waiting to pounce on any unremitting foe. For all practical purposes, the fate of the tribes had been sealed in the midst of winter at the hands of Edmund Andros, and it is no wonder that Puritan writers typically ignored the

---

[119] Ibid., 41.
[120] "Letter from Gov. Andros to the Deputy Governour of Connecticut, in King Phillip's Indian War, Hough, ed., 89.

episode in both reports and narratives. Cut off from any possibility of hope, and now surrounded on all sides by enemies, Metacomet and his people were determined to press on, even with a vision of ultimate defeat looming ahead.

Not surprisingly, with winter passing and Governor Andros waiting with his superior forces under his wing, the Puritans of New England stepped up their campaign to defeat the combined forces under Metacomet. Spring in New England found the Puritan forces prepared to sweep across the region to hunt down Metacomet's forces and cut them off from their food supply. Metacomet's people, however, continued to attack ever closer to the base of Puritan power in Boston. Towns such as Sudbury, Lancaster, Chelmsford, and many others were devastated by furious attacks by tribal forces during the spring, and although the English forces exacted the far greater toll in lost lives upon the Native Americans, the rebel forces persisted in engaging the desperate communities, and forcing many to greatly reduce their activities. One must realize that even as the Native Americans persisted in their attacks, their crops were not being planted, and their lands were securely in the hands of the English. Still, even as the weather warmed, Metacomet's forces turned upon the upper Connecticut River Communities with ferocious attacks against Pawcumtuck, Hadley, Springfield, and others. Again, large tolls upon the Native American attackers did not seem to abate the intensity of the war, instead only serving to increase the sense of desperation on both sides.

By the summer of 1676, however, many Native Americans headed back to their homelands only to find them occupied by armed forces. By the end of summer, the deaths of Weetamoo and Metacomet signaled the end for the rebellion, except for those Native Americans who managed to escape north into Maine, finding refuge in the territory once presided over by Samoset.

As this victory was sensed, the Puritan clergy evidently blundered in their first explanations and interpretation of what had turned out to be a complete disaster, a victory without any fruits other than the condemnation and criticism of their peers. Thus, blame for the war and the death and suffering of Puritan settlers became a petty religious exercise with little connection to the reality of why people were killed. The preachers had a better tactic – blaming it on the people's sins. This

Hidden Genocide, Hidden People

finger pointing in turn led to morbid consternation, manifesting itself in religious observances such as fasts and expressions of public forgiveness and humiliation. Thus they were sorry for their own sins, but none of those sins seemed in any way related to the brutality of war and the treatment of Native Americans. Another observance was invented in response, "a day of thanksgiving", something we in our modern age continue to practice, without true understanding of the origins of such celebrations. Perry Miller recounts the clergy's words and logic:

> In King Philip's War, repeated humiliations were followed by disasters, but the clergy had a ready explanation: the people had not sufficiently humbled themselves. ...The ministers' cry for more and more days of humiliation had reached a crescendo when, in June 1676, as the Native Americans were at long last checked, a secular insight proved to be in closer rapport with the will of God.[121]

Of course, modern historians tend to strongly reject attributions imposed upon extraordinary events as signs of God's favor or disfavor. But for the Puritans, every loss and every gain required a theological explanation. Even in the face of the war and associated deprivations, some Puritan leaders continued to believe that their mission was explainable through the typological framework of the exodus and the conquest of Canaan. But it broke down. Once the paradigm was established, the meanings of events had to fall within the parameters of logical explanation imposed by the model. It has been the same for many tyrannical regimes throughout the history of the world. The Puritans, however, were one of the worst, setting in motion an ongoing genocidal war that did not let up until all Native Americans eventually either disappeared or acquiesced to the horrific conditions imposed upon them in defeat, including slavery and ongoing persecution. In this paradigm, there was no room for mercy nor rational thinking because it all accorded with their god's plan.

Thus Increase Mather would write following the war without evidence of a pang of remorse nor any sense of accountability:

> ...But God hath consumed them by the Sword, and by Famine and by Sickness, it being no unusual

The King Phillip War and Genocide

thing for those that traverse the woods to find dead Native Americans up and down, who either Famine, or sickness, hath caused to dy, and there hath been none to bury them."[122]

...Now here it is to be observed, that God himself by his own hand brought this enemy to destruction.[123]

---

[121] Perry Miller. The New England Mind (Cambridge, MA :The Belknap Press of Harvard University Press: 1953), 22.
[122] Mather, The History of King Philip's War, 205.
[123] Ibid., 191.

Epilogue
Hidden People

Brothers, you see this vast country before us, which the great Spirit gave to our fathers and us; you see the buffalo and deer that now are our support. Brothers, you see those little ones, our wives and children, who are looking to us for food and raiment; and you now see the foe before you, that they have grown insolent and bold; that all our ancient customs are disregarded; the treaties made by our fathers and us are broken and all of us insulted; our council fires disregarded, all the ancient customs of our fathers; our brothers murdered before our eyes, and their spirits cry to us for revenge. Brothers, these people from the unknown world will cut down our groves, spoil our hunting and planting grounds, and drive us and our children from the graves of our fathers, and our council fires, and enslave our women and children.[124] *[attributed to Metacomet (King Philip) in 1835 by Rev. William Apess, Pequot, of Mashpee, Massachusetts]*

How deep, then, was the thought of Philip, when he could look from Maine to Georgia, and from the ocean to the lakes, and view with one look all his brethren withering before the more enlightened to come; and how true his prophecy, that the white people would not only cut down their groves but would enslave them. Had the inspiration of Isaiah been there, he could not have been more correct. Our groves and hunting grounds are gone, our dead are dug up, our council fires are put out, and a foundation was laid in the first Legislature to enslave our

---

[124] William Apess, "Eulogy on King Philip, as Pronounced at the Odeon, In Federal Street, Boston, 1836", in <u>The Complete Writings of William Apess</u>, Barry O'Connell, ed. (Amhearst: The University of Massachusetts Press, 1992), 295.

> people, by taking from them all rights, which has been strictly adhered to ever since. Look at the disgraceful laws, disenfranchising us as citizens. Look at the treaties made by Congress, all broken. A fire, a canker, created by the Pilgrims from across the Atlantic; to burn and destroy my poor unfortunate brethren, and it cannot be denied.[125] *[The Rev. William Apes in 1836 at the Odeon Theatre in Boston]*

At the end of the King Philip War, Puritan leaders were faced with a clear moral choice, namely, how to deal with the surviving captives, many of whom were non-combatant women and children. This dilemma was not easily resolved by the preachers, magistrates and theologians. Should one punish an innocent child or an innocent adult for the perceived wrongs of others and, if so, on what basis? There is no specific rule for this in the Bible, but there are many stories in which certain ideas might take root to elicit a typological comparison. The Puritans never refuted the "New Israel" justification of their mission, even if unexpected events had clouded their sense of eschatology and temporal certainty. With the end of the King Philip War, John Eliot's assertion that the Native Americans were actually Jewish had become scripturally untenable. In Eliot's theology, Native Americans from eastern Massachusetts were expected to spark a world revival because they would be the 'first fruits' – the beginning of a mass conversion of Jews that would spread first to the 'holy land' and then beyond. However, the unexpected great destruction brought upon the Christianized "Jewish" Native Americans cried out for another theological interpretation, a new paradigm to dispense with the guilt, pain and suffering that the war had brought to New England.

The Puritans created a considerable amount of literature in the decades preceeding the King Philip war, much of it portraying Native Americans as devil worshipers, the very incarnation of evil. It was this theological force which informed the Puritan conscience and moral behavior toward the Native Americans. Every violent act or atrocity committed by Native Americans gave the Puritans fuel for the fire. Sadly, it did not occur to the Puritans that wrongdoing on their own part might

---

[125] Ibid., **306**.

have given the Native Americans cause to react. "So like were these barbarous creatures to him who was a liar from the beginning.", Mary Rowlandson would write after her captivity at the hands of Wampanoags.[126] It is understandable that Rowlandson would perceive Native Americans as evil, considering her fate as a captive of Metacomet's forces. Her words reveal the impact that Puritan theology had upon her personally. Thus while Rowlandson certainly had rightful cause to complain about the treatment she received, she understood her captivity as part of a vast supernatural drama. The indignity and suffering imposed upon her would even become a rationale for greater brutalties against Native Americans in the future, the unfortunate legacy of her writings. Puritan policy was dictated by these convictions, and they provided an excuse for horrific genocidal acts such as the Narragansett Swamp Massacre, the Deer Island imprisonment, and a host of other actions that seem brutal by 20th-century standards, but even divinely ordered in the 17th.

Nevertheless, as the war came to an end, there were some who courageously stepped forward as advocates for the survivors; one of those was John Eliot, arguing his case against blanket executions and the policy of selling innocent Native Americans into slavery at the sugar plantations in the tropics, a fate worse than death in his estimation. The following is a sample portion from Eliot's petition on this question, written in the days preceding the final battles:

> To the Honorable the Governor & council, sitting at Boston this 13th of the 6th [August] [16]75 the humble petition of John Eliot Showeth: That the terror of selling away such Native Americans, unto the Islands for perpetual slaves, who shall yield up themselves to your mercy, is like to be an effectual prolongation of the war & such an exasperation of them, as may produce, we know not what evil consequence, upon all the land. Christ hath said, blessed are the merciful, for they shall obtain mercy. This usage of them is worse than death. To put to death men that

---

[126] Mary Rowlandson, The Captivity of Mary Rowlandson, ., in <u>A Critical Edition of Mrs. Mary Rowlandson's Captivity Narrative</u>, Robert Kent Diebold, ed. (Ph.D. diss., Yale University, 1972), 45.

Epilogue

have deserved to die, is an ordinance of God, & a blessing is promised to it. It may be done in faith. The design of Christ in these last days, is not to extirpate nations, but to gospelize them.[127]

Eliot's interpretations of the gospel mandate did not square with the imperatives found in the typology of Mather, who was the driving theological force throughout the war. Eliot's notion that the Native Americans could be "saved" was evidently too optimistic a viewpoint for those times. This is clearly evident in a comparison with Mather's suggestion on how to deal with the Native Americans at the end of the war, who rather callously advocated for a policy of extermination that included the enslavement or execution of the children of the vanquished tribes. Mather writes:

And indeed there is one sad consideration which may cause humble tremblings to think of it, namely, in that the Reformation which god expects from us is not so hearty and so perfect as it ought to be, Divines observe, that whereas upon Samuel's Exhortation, the people did make but imperfect work of it, as to the Reformation of provoking evils, therefore God did only begin their deliverance by Samuel, but left scattered Philistines unsubdued, who afterwards made head and proved a sore scourge to the children of Israel, until David's time, in whose Reign there was a full Reformation, and then did the Lord give unto his people full deliverance.[128]

Many people would be shocked by the official extermination policies enacted in colonial New England during the King Philip War and its aftermath show. The policies alone show that Puritan brutality toward Native Americans was excessive, harsh and unwavering in general. The reason they acted in such a nefarious manner is clear – the presumed righteousness of the Puritan cause. One incident demonstrates why so many Native Americans fled in the aftermath to Maine and Canada for protection. George Bodge describes the incident and

---

[127] Segal and Stineback, <u>Puritans, Indians & Manifest Destiny</u>, 204.
[128] Mather, <u>The History of the King Philip's War</u>, 205-206.

its consequence:

> These Native Americans suffered a great outrage at the hands of some English Native American-haters, who upon the burning of a barn of Lieut. Richardson at Chelmsford by some skulking hostile Native Americans, immediately and without authority assaulted these helpless Wamesits, wounding five women and children, and killing outright a lad, wounding his mother, dauthter of Sagamore John and widow of another sagamore. "Tohatoonee," a true friend of the English. ... It was by such outrages as these that those Native Americans who inclined to peace were alienated, and those already inclined to war embittered,... Many of the young men fled to northern groups such as the Ammoscoggins and Pequakets and others. These Native Americans were led by one Squando who had become angry at the treatment of his wife and child by English sailors. These sailors, it is said, seeking to test the common report that Native American children could swim naturally, like the young of beasts, maliciously upset the canoe containing the woman and child; the child sank in the river, but the mother diving to the bottom saved it, which, however, soon after dying, its death was imputed to this treatment.[129]

By most military measures, the War had been a stunning victory, but it was a bittersweet success for the winners. Many of the soldiers who had been conscripted were promised grants of land as remuneration for their participation, but at war's end, there was no booty for those who had fought. In fact, the United Colonies were in political and economic shambles; close to fifteen percent of the English population had been killed and the food production capacity of the colonies was depleted, and worse, Puritan rule itself was threatened by the royalist government. The War had indeed not furthered nor favored Puritan interests. Charles Segal and David Stineback provide an analysis of the

---

[129] George Madison Bodge, Soldiers in King Philip's War, (Leominister, MA: Printed for the author, 1896) 300-301.

Epilogue

diplomatic events after the war which would lead to the dissolution of Puritan theocracy:

> ...Edward Randolph, arrived in Boston to find and expose the vices of Puritan rule. Among other charges that Randolph relayed to the mother country was the accusation that Puritans in general, not the Pilgrims of Plimoth Colony in particular, had provoked the war by harassing Metacom and selling liquor and arms to the Native Americans.[130]

It was clear just who was the winner within a few short years. In 1684, the Massachusetts Bay Charter was revoked by James II. And like every great empire which has brought about its own demise, the final days of the Puritan empire were ones of considerable internal power struggles. Under the weight of imminent collapse, the theological certainty of earlier Puritans began to wane, and there followed a period of intensified self-castigation over the failure of the Puritan mission itself. But it didn't remain dormant for long. The apocalytic and millenial beliefs of the seventeenth century still punctuate the public discourse today. Whether witch trials, massacres or physical tortures, the Puritan penchant for religious triumphalism and the associated xenophobia has remained and is still embedded in the national identity.

The self-castigation of Puritans never extended so far as to question Puritan policies against the Native Americans, and that lack of accountability is still strong today. In America, few connect the fate of Native Americans who currently reside elsewhere. That is because the Puritans proudly proclaimed their victory and the righteousness of their cause There was no shame. Even those Puritans who expressed regret over the oppression of religious dissenters during that period seemed rather blind to the injustices perpetuated against Native Americans, and their descendants marched right on in their footsteps. Why is it such a forgotten episode still? Perhaps it is because few in that day felt a need for forgiveness, nor wanted to be reminded of the cruelties adminstered in the name of religion. Perhaps it is found in these conciliatory words, written by a settler named Richard Hutchin-

---

[130] Charles and Stineback, Puritans, Indians, & Manifest Destiny, 215

son, appealing for collective self-pardon:

> We have been, and still are ready to put different Reflections upon the Murders and Spoils that have been made upon us by this Destructive War: Various are Mens Thoughts why God hath suffered it, all acknowledge it was for Sin: many wish there hath not been some Leaven of the Spirit in the Provocation for which we left Old England. I am in great Pain while I write, to remember how severe some of us have been to Dissenters, making Spoil without Pity, but god is teaching us Moderation.[131]

Hutchinson seems to be simplifying a complex phenomenon and missing vital elements in thinking that if only his people could have been more moderate, they wouldn't have caused so much suffering in the war. He may be right in his analysis, but wrong in his conclusion. The truth is that moderation is meaningless without wisdom to guide it, and wisdom is impossible without a clear understanding of justice. That is the contradictory element in Puritanism. The Puritan way stressed obedience to the Mosaic law codes of ancient Israel, but was blind to the injustice of their treatment of the Native Americans. The blindness was not a result of strict obedience to the law, but a result based upon an errant typological interpretation of the conquests of ancient Israel. Beyond that model, New England Puritanism could not exist. Thus when the end of the King Philip War resulted in the end of Puritan government, the theological foundations upon which it had been built collapsed. But the negative myth of the Native American which it created did not die.

While the typological foundation that undergirded Puritan expansion eroded with the loss of the charter, certain of its elements lived on, albeit in a modified secular form. Thus the myth justified westward expansion in later centuries, when, under the banner of "manifest destiny", European immigrants pushed their way across the continent. The theological certainty which fueled Puritan conquest was thus altered and adapted to fit new secular circumstances, to explain and interpret new wars, and justify new persecutions. The theologically based

---

[131] Richard Hutchinson, "The Warr in New England Visibly Ended", in <u>Narratives of the Indian Wars</u>, Charles H. Lincoln, ed., p. 103.

Epilogue

negative myth of the Native American was transformed into a broad set of attitudes which gave impetus to the vast conquests waged across the North American continent. But the myth itself was not changed; it merely turned on a new theological axis.

The negative myth of the Native American did not die because it was planted in the collective unconscious of this nation at its inception. Few Americans of European descent would question, even today, the assertion that the United States has a special 'spiritual birthright' with a divine mission. The Puritans did \not question the validity of their mission or covenant with their god, only their ability to fulfill it. They saw their fate as a specific plan predestined by their god, and revealed in direct comparisons of their experiences to Hebrew people in the Bible. This was their Exodus! To disown that claim would have raised unanswerable and unapproachable questions about their beliefs and actions, specifically genocide. Under this conviction, the experiment had to go forth and the Puritans could not revise their positions. But as the experiment proceeded, escalating rhetoric and actions seemed to be required in order to protect its outcome. And in the end, the conquests of America were almost always defined in terms of the 'negative myth' of the Native American. The myth lived on, but so did the Native Americans in New England. Impoverished, persecuted, and hidden from sight, the scattered remnants of Algonquin survivors struggled to maintain their existance and way of life in the face of insurmountable public opposition, even to this day.

In 1835, William Apess, a Methodist minister and native-born Pequot, visited the Wampanoag town of Mashpee on Cape Cod. The Mashpee Wampanoags of that town had been sorely oppressed for many years by its appointed overseers from Harvard University, a group called the Williams Committee, responsible for governance and disbursement of finances for the town. For many years, the committee had allowed abuses and profiting off Mashpee land and while leaving little for the impoverished Mashpees. During his visit, Apess was asked by a group of Mashpees to assist them in gaining legal control of their land and religion as a means of raising themselves up from their degraded and impoverished existence. Apess, readily agreeing, quickly put a plan into action, including leading a delegation to Boston in order to present a petition to the General Court.

Hidden Genocide, Hidden People

In 1835, travel to Boston was a difficult place for Native Americans, and Apess recounts the humiliation of not being able to find suitable lodging in the city because of their skin color, offering up his own typological comparison inspired by the experiences:

> We regarded ourselves, in some sort, as a tribe of Israelites suffering under the rod of despotic pharoahs; for thus far, our cries and remonstrances had been of no avail. We were compelled to make our bricks without straw. We now in our synagogue, for the first time, concerted the form of a government, suited to the spirit and capacity of freeborn sons of the forest after the pattern set us by our white brethren. There was but one exception, viz., that all who dwelt in our precincts were to be held free and equal, in truth, as well as in letter.[132]

Apess's words demonstrate the irony of typology; as a method of Biblical interpretation, it can be used to support any number of competing, conflicting, and even contradictory views. In demonstrating how those typological understandings contributed to the creation of the 'negative myth of the Indian', the extermination of Native American civilizations and the censoring of this record from history books, this study has demonstrated the dangers of typology and theological triumphalism. However, Apess demonstrates the positive potential of typology, enabling the believer to stretch forth the religious imagination in order to find meaning in history. But that meaning can never be fixed, nor can it be used to justify brutality in the name of a god or gods. Apess demonstrates its true power. Using the typological symbols and rhetoric of his oppressors, Apess could readily exult even in the midst of trials and tribulations, declaring in words reminiscent of those who used them with violence and persecution against his ancestors the following affirmation of hope for his people:

> Oh when shall the sweet voice of mercy reach all
> my kindred according to the flesh! When shall the

---

[132] Apess, William, "Indian Nullification of the Unconstitutional Laws of Massachusetts Relative to the Marshpee Tribe"; or, "The Pretended Riot Explained (1835)", in On Our Own Ground, the Complete Writings of William Apess, 179.

desert break out into songs of praise, loud and high, like the lion cry of Judah's warriors in their day of triumph! When shall the proud, strong, and fleet warriors of the western wilds, the remnants of powerful tribes, come up to the help of the Lord against the man of sin, as strong and as bold for Christ as they are in council, and in deeds of arms! Let us pray for Zion…and let us remember her scattered and peeled people in their sorrowful season of desertion. The lamp of Israel shall burn again, and the star of Judah shall rise again, never to go down, for it will shine over Bethelehem. [133]

---

[133] William Apess, "The Increase of the Kingdom of Christ", in On Our Own Ground, the Complete Writings of William Apess, 107.

Index

Algonquin 3, 9, 10-11, 16, 42-44, 78, 86, 108-114, 116-124, 134, 144, 162
Andros, Edmund 101, 151-153
Antinomian 59, 83
Apess, Rev. William 156-157, 163, 164-165

Basheba(s) 23
Basque(s) 37, 18-31
Baylie, Rev. Robert 103
Bourne, Richard 122
Bradford, William 20, 23, 25, 80, 84

Cabot, John Sebastian 13
Cambridge 34
Champlain, Samuel 16, 26
Canonicus 66, 99, 114, 130
Cape Nedick, Maine 29
Cartier, Jacque 17
Casco 23
Castell, William 7
Charlestown 34
Chickatabot 42
Coke, Sir Edward 93
Commissioners of the United Colonies 148
Conant, Roger 34
Cotton, John 3,4,36,48,70,86,92-94,106,136
Cotton Code 2-3, 96-97
Cromwell, Oliver 112, 128
Cutshamequin 89, 109-220, 114-115

Devil 5, 39, 77, 105, 115, 116, 124-128, 156
Donnacona 18
Dorchester Mill 116
Dyer, Mary 2

Eliot John, 36, 59, 60, 61, 71, 103, 106-107, 109, 110-120, 123, 127-129, 139, 145, 159, 151, 152, 157, 159
Endicott, John   34, 39

Gardener, Lion 81
Genocide 1, 11,13, 14, 46, 76, 94-95, 100, 136,146
Gilbert, Bartolomew 29

Gookin, Daniel 3, 108, 118, 130, 149
Gorges, Sir Ferdinando 14, 16, 24, 32, 47, 58,
Gorton, Samuel 91, 98-99, 108, 115
Gosnold, Captain Bartolomew 29

Hadley 153
Hartford 44, 53-54, 71, 85, 89, 91, 101, 153
Harvard College (University) 82, 121, 162
Hooker, Thomas 60, 62, 65,
Hubbard, William 136-137, 147-148
Hunt, Thomas 19
Hutchinson, Anne 2, 50, 59, 70, 82
Hutchinson, Richard, 161-162

Iroquois 13

Johnson, Edward 40, 115

King James 17
King Philip War 11, 25, 88, 98, 101, 112, 121, 127, 129, 136, 137, 145-146, 149, 150, 157, 159, 162

Lancaster 153
Lescarbot, Marc 26
Levett, Christopher 23

Massachusetts Bay 3, 13, 34, 38, 46-73, 85-92, 99-105, 109, 111, 117, 120, 128, 133, 134, 143-146, 149, 161,
Massachusetts Bay Company 3, 34, 38, 40, 48

Index

Massachusetts (tribe) 34, 41, 42, 45
Massachusetts General Court 45, 54, 89, 116, 118, 120, 128, 154, 163
Massasoit 97, 132,
Morton, Thomas 10, 14, 15, 42, 60, 114
Moseley, Captain Samuel 149-150
Mason, Captain John 94-95, 72, 76-78
Mather, Increase 37, 129, 138, 139, 140, 145, 146, 155, 160

Maverick, Samuel 102,
Mayhew, Thomas 121
Mawooshen 20, 22-25, 31-32
Merrymount 15
Metacomet (King Phillip) 126, 132, 134-236, 139, 143, 151, 156, 158
Miantonomo 66, 67, 89, 90-91, 93, 99, 101, 109
Mohegan (tribe) 33, 62, 73, 85, 88, 90, 91, 99-100
Mount Wachusett 151

Nanapashemet 32
Narragansett (tribe) 10, 37, 43, 48-52, 56, 61, 65-101
Nipmuc (tribe) 32, 87, 121-122, 124, 145-146, 148,
Naumkeag 54
New Haven 3, 101,
Nonantum 116, 117, 119-121

Omen 1, 83, 95, 153
Oldham, John 47, 61, 65, 67, 69

Pauwau 109, 110, 114, 117-118, 125-127
Penacook(s) 89, 122, 123, 147,
Pasconoway 89
Pequot 22, 36-39, 42-43, 52-58, 60-97, 102, 104, 114-115, 156, 159, 162-163
Pequot war 11, 67-68, 77-78, 82, 88-89, 94-95, 102, 105, 115
Pilgrim(s) 8, 15-17, 21, 33, 53, 158, 161
Piumbukho 123-125

Plimoth Company 16, 24, 46
Pocumtuck(s) 86
Pokenoket(s) 20
Pomham 108
Praying towne 108, 110, 112-113, 116, 120, 144, 146, 148, 150, 157

Quinnipiac 83

Rhode Island 31, 34, 48, 51, 60, 67, 67, 89, 101, 107, 108, 129-133, 139, 152
Rowlandson, Mary 154-155
Roxbury 34

Saco 24
Sacononocco 198
Samoset 19, 20, 22-27, 32
Sassious (Sassacus) 62-65
Sassamon 127
Sasanoa 31
Saybrook Company 53, 59, 63, 65-69
Shawomet 108
Simmons, William 5
Squanto 19-22
Standish, Myles 24, 100
Star Chamber 148
Stone, Captain John 56-57, 60, 64-66,
Sudbury 153

Tarratine(s) 23, 24-32
Theocracy 2, 3, 62, 160,
Thorowgood, Rev. Thomas 111
Tihanedo 24
Typology/Typological 4, 7, 36, 37, 40, 46, 94, 95, 97, 138, 145, 146, 153, 157, 159, 162-164

Uncas 62

Index

Verrazzano, Giovanni 13

Waban 113, 116
Wampanoag 10,14,100,114,122,128,130,122-126,142-144,148, 158,
Warwick 98-99
Western Niantics 56, 61, 65, 85,
Weymouth George 139
Winslow, Governor Edward 24
Winthrop, Jr. John 65
Williams, Roger 2, 8, 10, 26, 27, 48, 58, 60, 66, 68, 70, 72, 74, 78, 88, 92, 96, 98, 102, 104, 106, 107, 126, 128, 130, 132
Wilson, Rev. John 84,138

View of Boston from Deer Island, the site where over 500 "Christianized" Native Americans were imprisoned without food and shelter in wintertime during the King Philip War.

Photo credit: Rachael Cerrotti

King Philip War monument in Templeton, Massachusetts. During the winter of 1676, a large force of soldiers was recruited to attack the Narragansetts. Many of the recruits were young men without land and resources, and were promised a parcel of land in return for their services. The Mass. Bay government did not honor the pledge until 1734 when a lawsuit resulted in the creation of seven "Narragansett" townships.

Thomas Sawin house in Natick. Thomas Sawin was hired by Natick Native Americans in 1692 to help them with building a mill and other structures after the King Philip War. They also gave him the land upon which the house he built remains to this day, although there are currently attempts to remove it to a different location.

King Philip Restaurant, Lounge and Motor Inn in Philipston RI. This landmark establishment commemorates the local area where Metacomet (King Philip) and thousands of Wampanoags, Nipmucs, Narragansetts, Massachusetts and other Native Americans survived the long winter of 1676 during the King Philip War.